AF480088
September
makes
a
mess
of
me

Also by Casey Merkley

An Eternity of Everythings
To taste you in another form

September makes a mess of me
Casey Merkley

Dear reader

I hope you find a bucket
and you fill it with so much love,
it overflows continuously.

So you'll always have a love bucket
like I do.

tear my laughter in two ,

find a place on my body soft er than

this know ing night .

let tight lips fall into rose y skin ,

touch this burn ing flesh

with rain on your breath .

glass boy with wild lips,
every kiss feels like a heavenly honey sun.
listen to my soft breath soar through tight ache.
warm hands bend deeply inside tender places,
an open mouth smiles skips this bare heart.
slowly drink this endless night.

a summer heart ache s for

a star to give birth to a danc ing night .

big silk y moon ,

do you give life to everything you

can taste ?

one hundred hungry moment s pour
into my mouth
laugh
& I feel my earth pull ing apart .
a warm heaven crawl s in to my reach
ocean
like it belong s ,
& for a bit ,
I
find
happiness .

4

tender lover , keep
this laughter between soft hand s ,
shed ache tomorrow .

let your finger s live

with in long whisper s that taste

like burn ing night time .

soft ness is

a summer sun feel ing for wild flower s

between breakfast & lunch ,

bend ing their bloom to the sky ,

ask ing for nothing .

soft ness is

when your lips grow lazy against mine ,

all flesh & star struck .

wild laughter cut s through my

gentle shape & we

do n't
go
quiet ly .

soft ness is
anything that stay s .

butterfly stomach,

meet me between blooming mouths

and sweet guiding hands.

soft ness is

a long embrace that

find s you when you ' re

not search ing .

taste each secret with hungry ,

delight ful hand s .

my soul , a ghost ly storm

to hold tender ly with two ...

touch

me

all

over .

of
this

soft ness is
different

it 's **pull** **ing** emotion **s** apart ,

a **slow** **ocean** .

a **sharp** , hungry Romance

it 's a **long** pour **ing** pray er

endless eyes

&

ask **ing** **for** **for** give n ess .

spring bird,

learning wind & world.

wild friend, sweep the sky with parted wings

& infinite ballads as soft as time will fall

from natures tender petals.

live within this bloom

this bare gaze.

soar between these lifetimes.

a swollen daffodil kiss es a **play** ful butterfly

on **the mouth** effortlessly .

a basket of clover s **fall** madly in love

with the birth of **spring** .

an eager tulip flirt s with a bee **and**

I rattle **like summer** thunder .

hungry **mouth** **,** **come** **quick**

burn **ing** lips part with ache to

swallow **this** whisper

amber eye s lay softly in a tender bed of August &

wrap this night around the summer sun .

sweat out this grow ing fever

shed your old self

& promise to stay .

glass boy with a child like love &

forever finger s

I am lost in your wild & your soft .

I am all lazy inside s and jolly and

you and I are infinite heart s carve d

from a crisp apple tree .

taste this cozy harvest , this tender mouth ,

lick these long ing thought s of you .

I am pastel pray er s

&

m i d night eyes .

a slow burn ing ocean

&

the wing s of a last breath .

you are a sweet feast

and

you laugh with your mouth open .

a tender bed of lips

and

flick er ing eye s ,

you are vast and endless

and

I am sure .

cranberry sunshine

a swollen **bloom** offer s her **self**

a crisp bed **of** gentle daisies **&** warm tulip **s** .

squeeze **the juicy** gold **&** yellow garden , swallow **flesh** y

berries , taste **the** bright spring **in your mouth** .

cloud s meet summer Day s

in **a** sweltering promise to always leave

shade for **those that** L i n g e r .

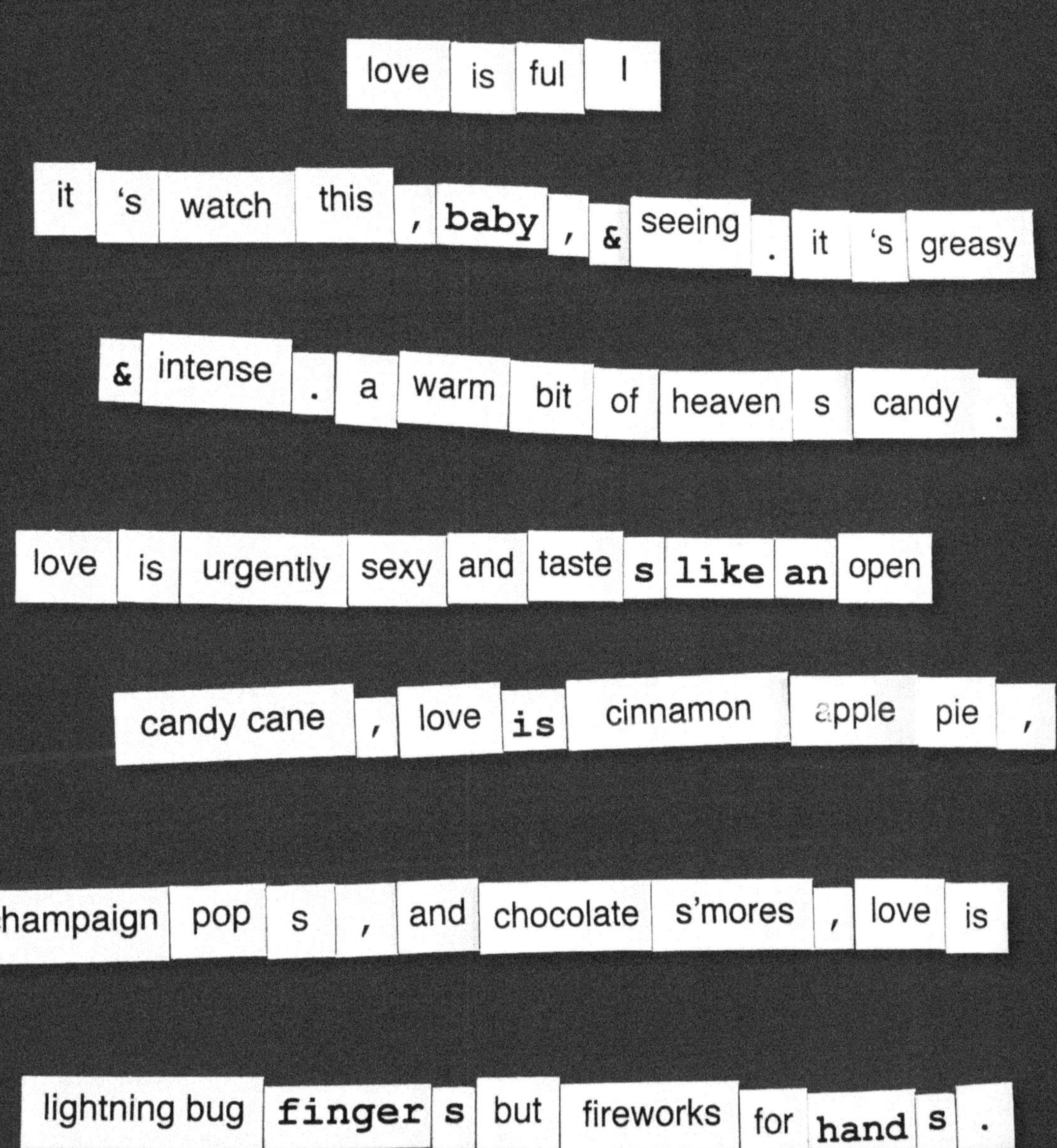

love is ful l

it 's watch this , baby , & seeing . it 's greasy

& intense . a warm bit of heaven s candy .

love is urgently sexy and taste s like an open

candy cane , love is cinnamon apple pie ,

champaign pop s , and chocolate s'mores , love is

lightning bug finger s but fireworks for hand s .

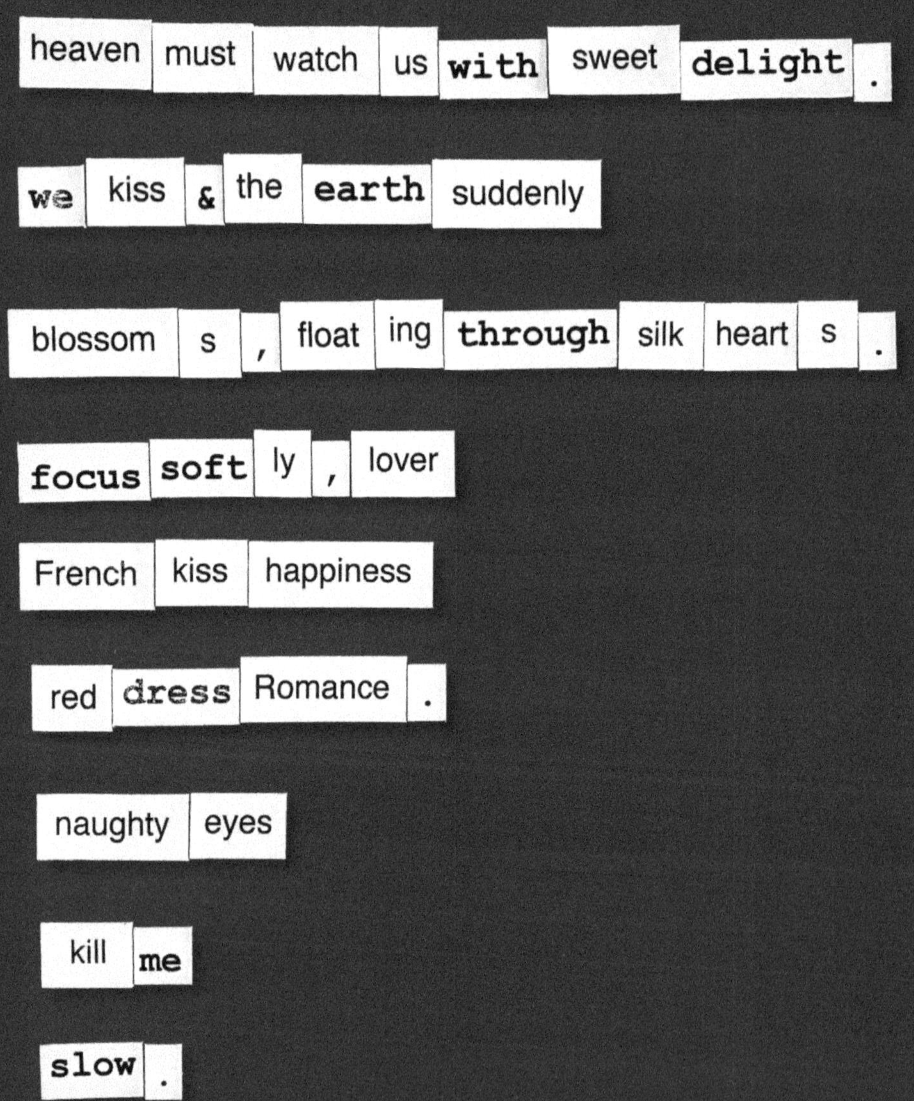

heaven must watch us with sweet delight .
we kiss & the earth suddenly
blossom s , float ing through silk heart s .
focus soft ly , lover
French kiss happiness
red dress Romance .
naughty eyes
kill me
slow .

love is

slurp these endless fingers with holy wine in your cheek s .

love is a golden burn turn ed icy with a rich undeniable

shiver in my stomach . love is ignite every wonder in my

body & turn laughter in to friction . love is grow ing

flesh under light rain and imagine find ing luck in

an open chest . love is lightning on a bare night

& thunder grasp ing the fever in your bone s .

love is a match only a name can freeze .

who was I ?

I was a long secret

a wild apology

a give anything girl

a bare summer sizzle

I was a come & go

a lazy whisper crawling in your mouth

I 'd wilt in your hand

&

peck at your fingers .

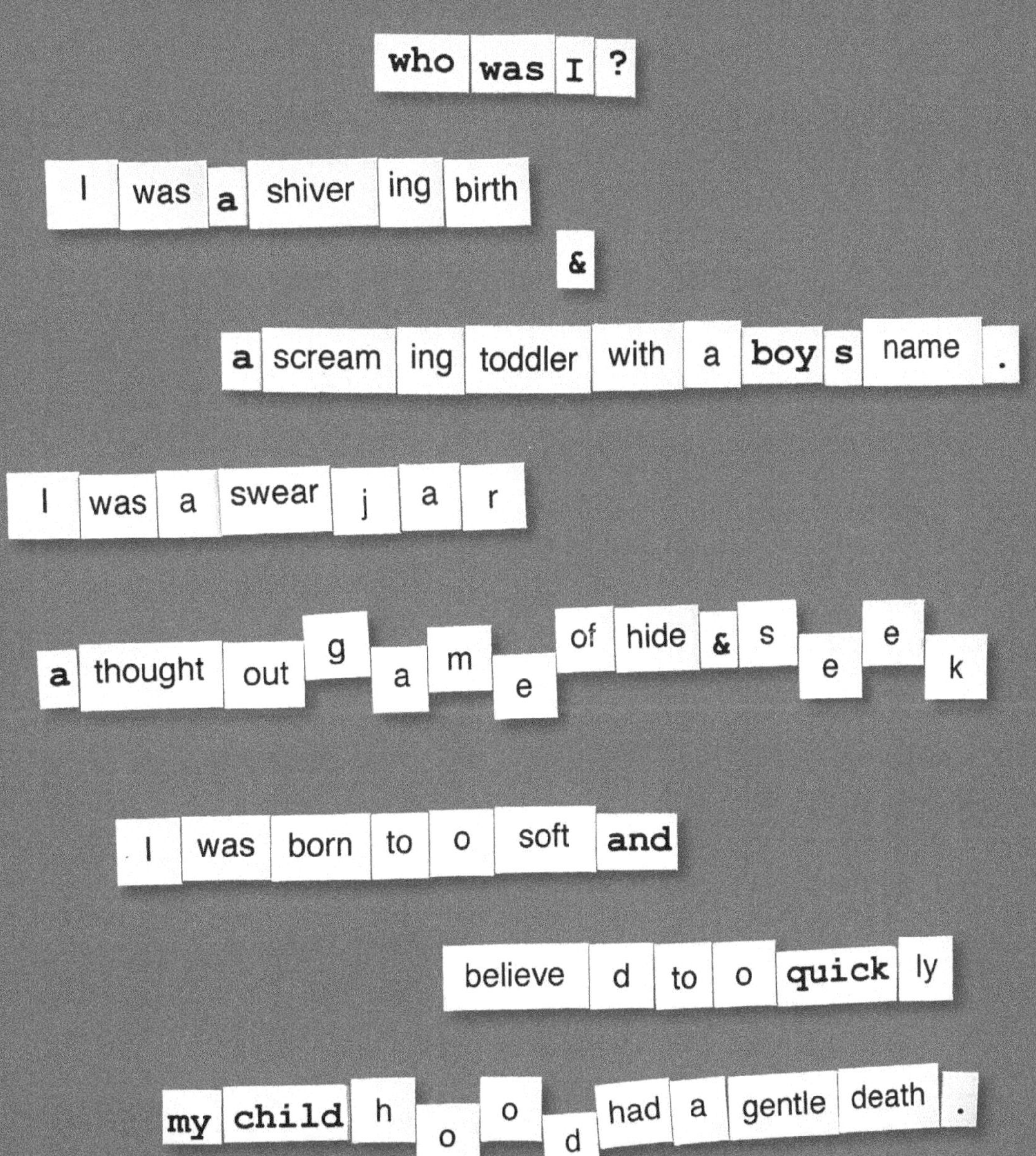

who was I ?
I was a shivering birth
&
a screaming toddler with a boys name.
I was a swear j a r
a thought out g a m e of hide & s e e k
I was born too soft and
believed too quickly
my childhood had a gentle death.

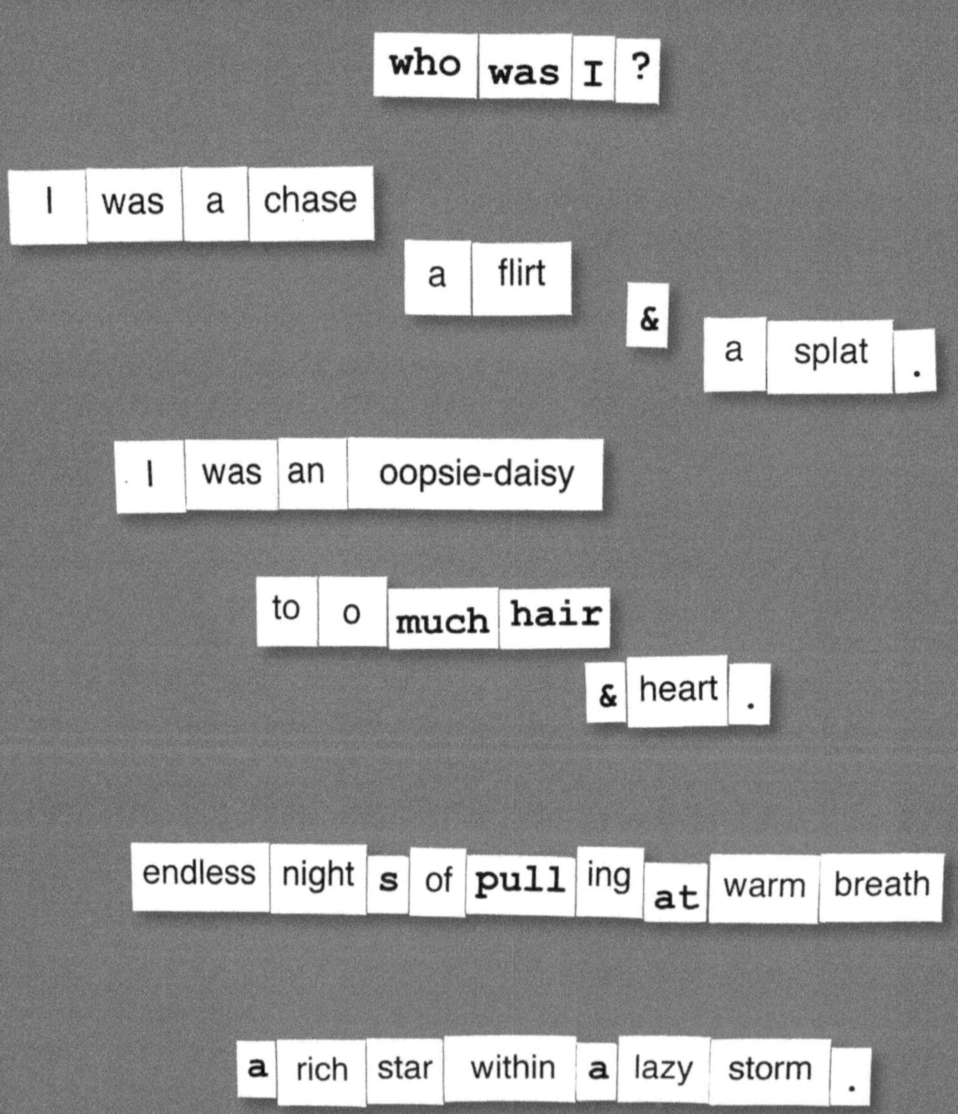

who was I ?
I was a chase
a flirt
&
a splat .
I was an oopsie-daisy
to o much hair
& heart .
endless night s of pull ing at warm breath
a rich star within a lazy storm .

who was I ?

I was the shape of a glass home .

a delicate tear met with an almost .

I was a look er

a win n ing smile

a tempt ing growl .

I was a lover wrap p ed in sweet wine

a naked heaven

& hell on my side .

you make me feel

different , alive

like an apple orchard fizz ing

like endless sunshine & long s t e m rose s .

like pour ing poetry in a plump champaign glass

like I could paint the earth green & pink

like sticky ice cream on top of play ful scream s

like I can carve my shadow from your thigh

and taste the proof .

hot girl shit

missing my Dr. appt to masturbate

collecting hearts with each aim

burying my first love with a soft no

and dead eyes

not waxing any lips , get wet or go home

flirting with him & her & them and you

skipping breakfast to swallow my appetite in

hard apple cider

asking strippers for skin care

routines

crotchless panties are not a phase

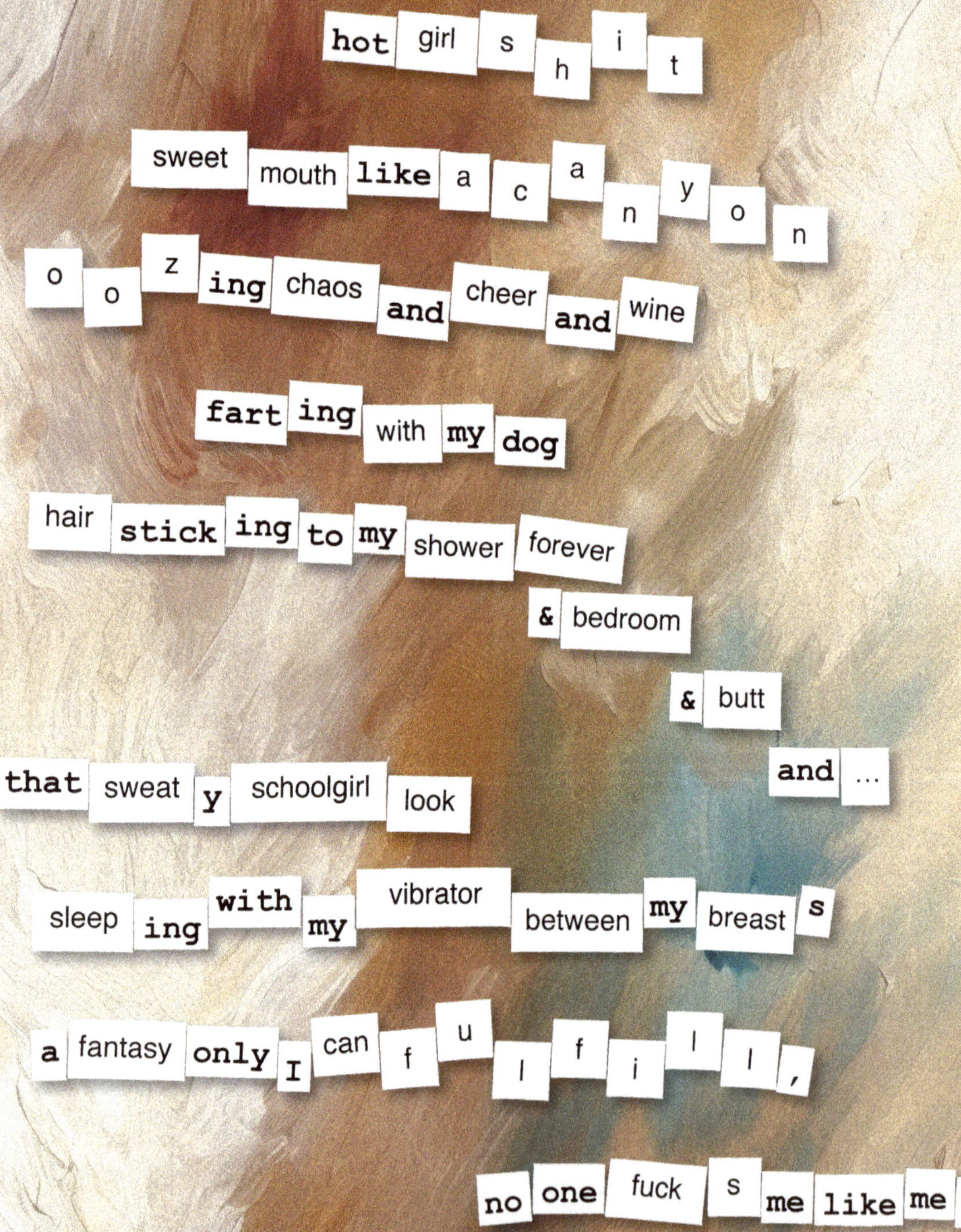

hot girl s h i t
sweet mouth like a c a n y o n
o o z ing chaos and cheer and wine
fart ing with my dog
hair stick ing to my shower forever
& bedroom
& butt
and …
that sweat y schoolgirl look
sleep ing with my vibrator between my breast s
a fantasy only I can f u l f i l l ,
no one fuck s me like me .

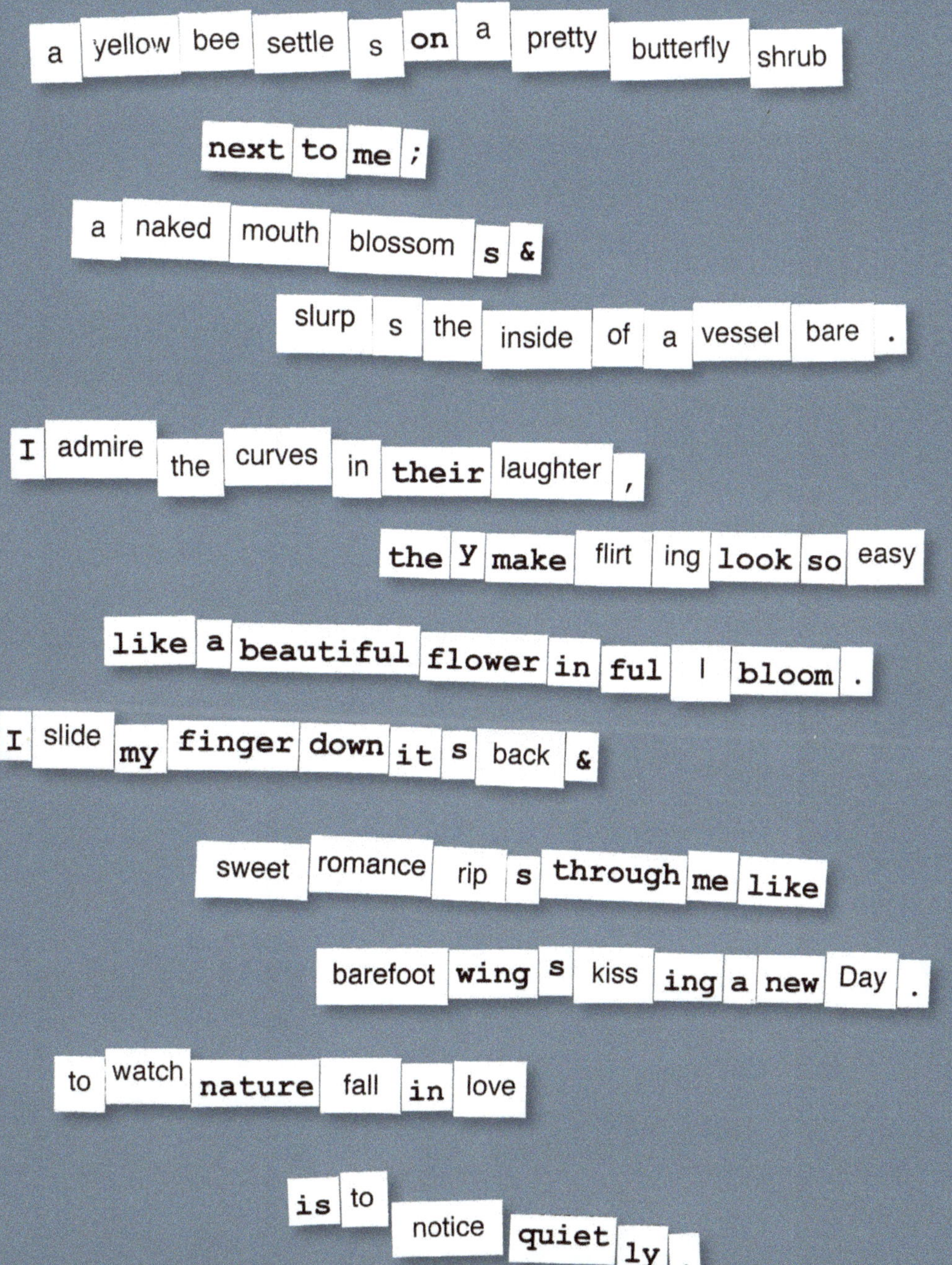

a yellow bee settle s on a pretty butterfly shrub
next to me ;
a naked mouth blossom s &
slurp s the inside of a vessel bare .
I admire the curves in their laughter ,
the y make flirt ing look so easy
like a beautiful flower in ful l bloom .
I slide my finger down it s back &
sweet romance rip s through me like
barefoot wing s kiss ing a new Day .
to watch nature fall in love
is to notice quiet ly .

when I die , celebrate me under French sunshine .

rip

meet my death with a sweet visit & a mood suck ing witness .

wrap me in a bed of wind & storm .

remember , I'm inside out .

be delicate .

sleep with my ghost , let her go down on you .

I keep feel ing the haunt , the reach ,

the distance of space ,

When will I feel the shock of living ?

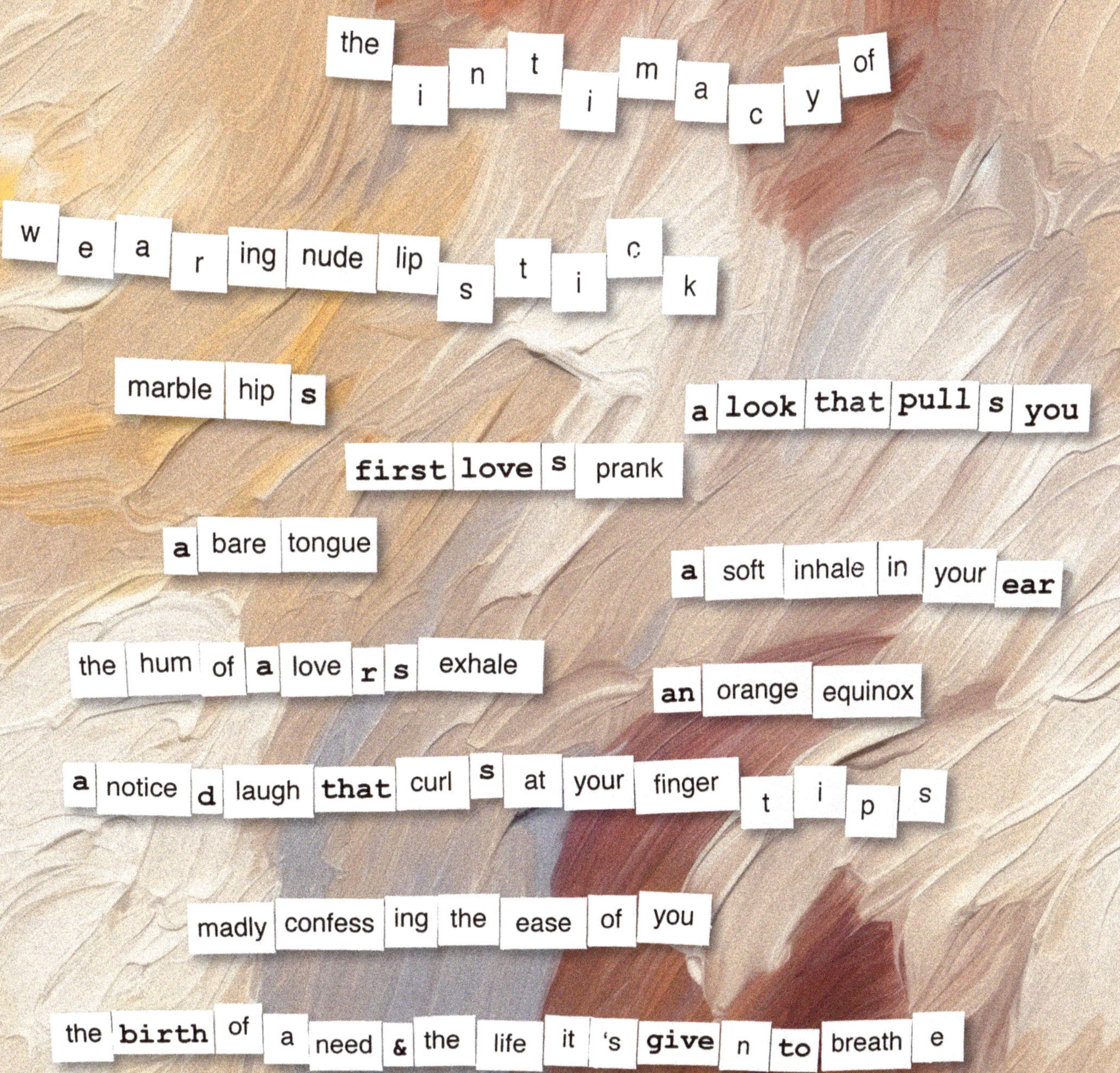

the intimacy of
wearing nude lipstick
marble hips
a look that pulls you
first loves prank
a bare tongue
a soft inhale in your ear
the hum of a lovers exhale
an orange equinox
a noticed laugh that curls at your fingertips
madly confessing the ease of you
the birth of a need & the life it's given to breathe

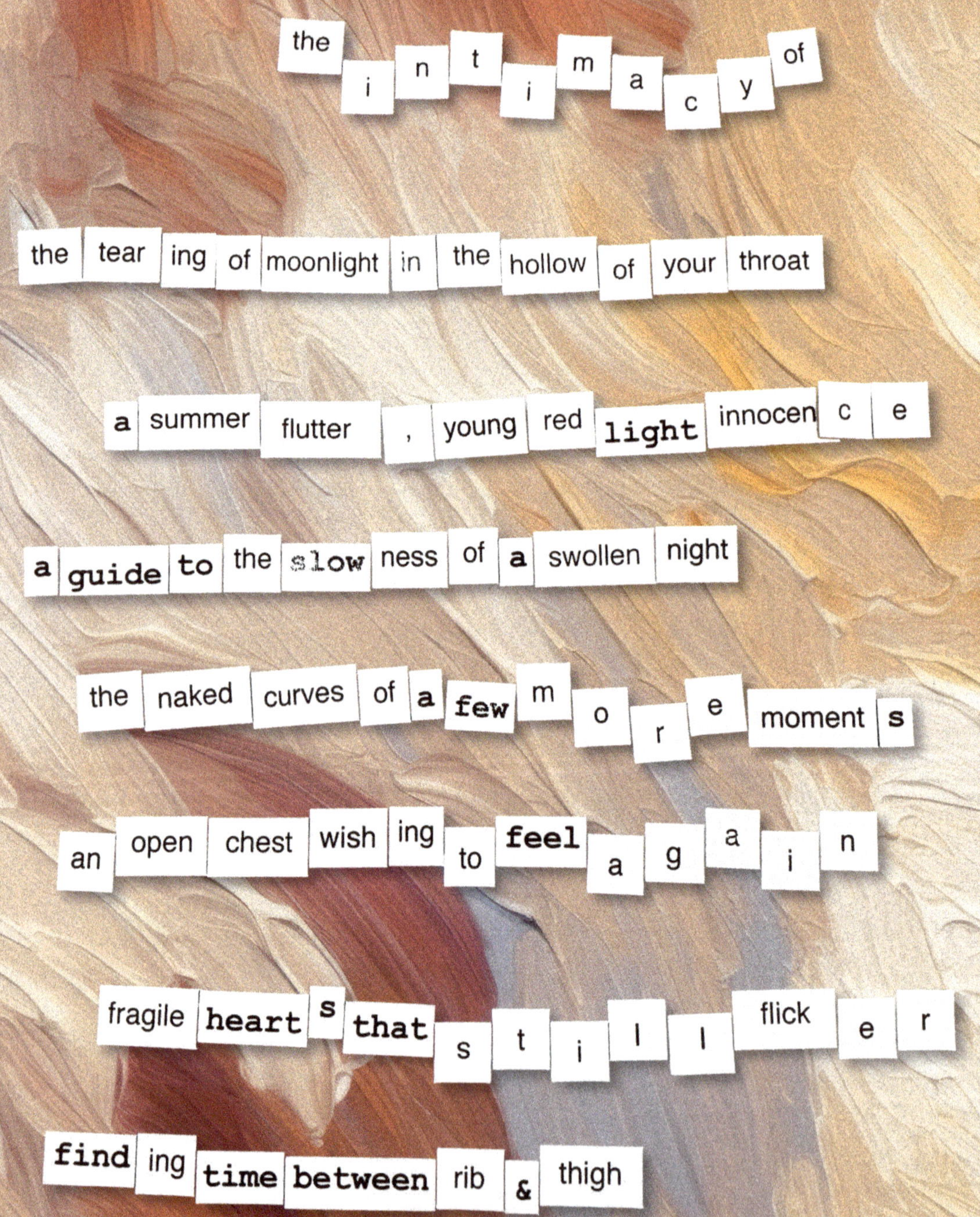

the intimacy of
the tear ing of moonlight in the hollow of your throat
a summer flutter , young red light innocence
a guide to the slow ness of a swollen night
the naked curves of a few more moment s
an open chest wish ing to feel again
fragile heart s that still flick er
find ing time between rib & thigh

if it 's not

bust ed open & plump , unconditional , daring to understand

& a heart strip p ed of ache .

nearly as challeng ing as me , all bang and boom ,

tempt ing me to truly give it my all .

easy go ing , uncanny , made to squirm and flutter .

if it 's not a sultry whisper shock ing my blood deep down ,

confess ing everything to the sky , watch tonight come ,

while tomorrow whimper s .

if it 's not my most pain ful goodbye ,

I don't want it .

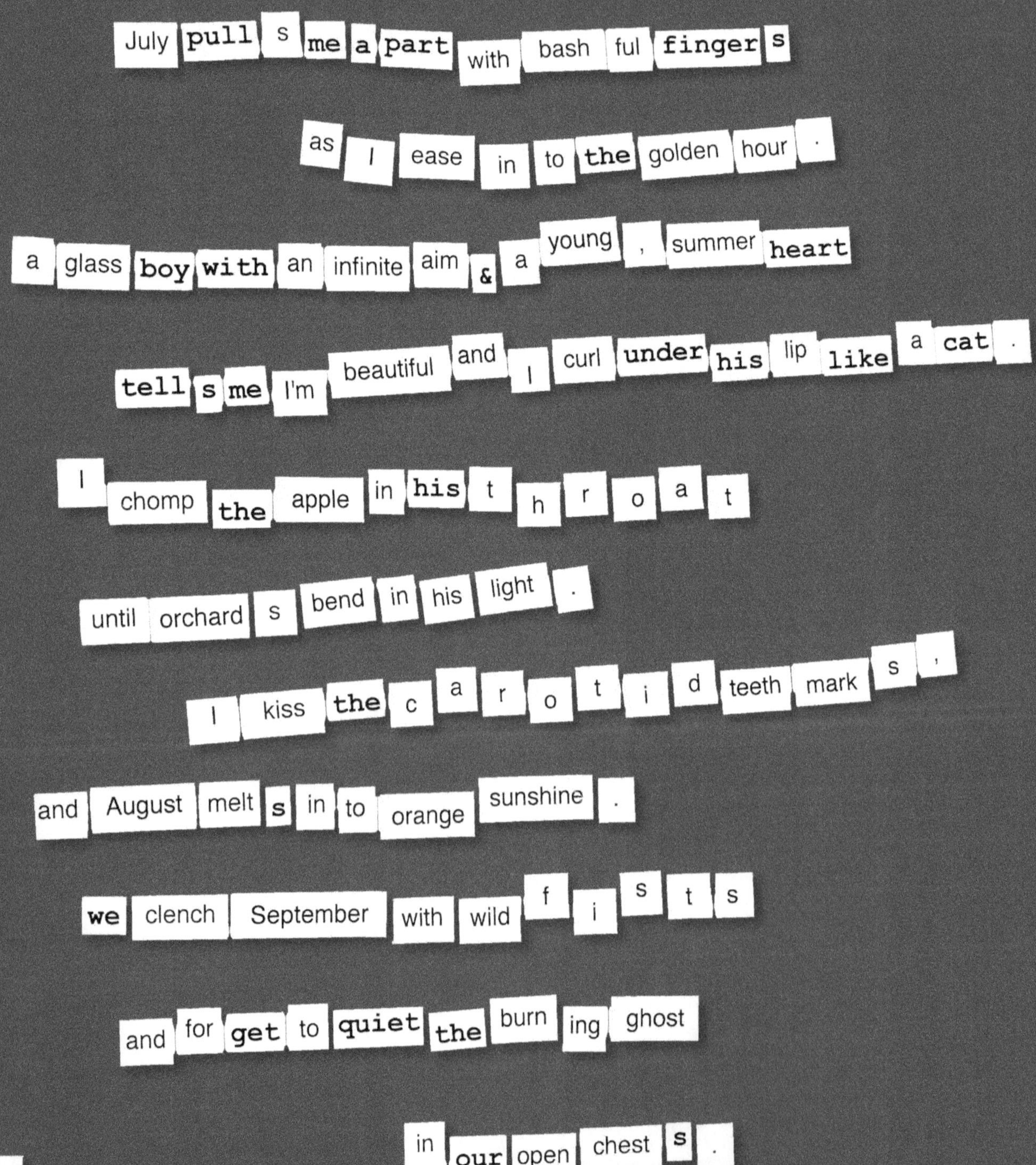

July pulls me apart with bashful fingers
as I ease in to the golden hour .
a glass boy with an infinite aim & a young , summer heart
tells me I'm beautiful and I curl under his lip like a cat .
I chomp the apple in his throat
until orchards bend in his light .
I kiss the carotid teeth marks ,
and August melts in to orange sunshine .
we clench September with wild fists
and forget to quiet the burning ghost
in our open chests .

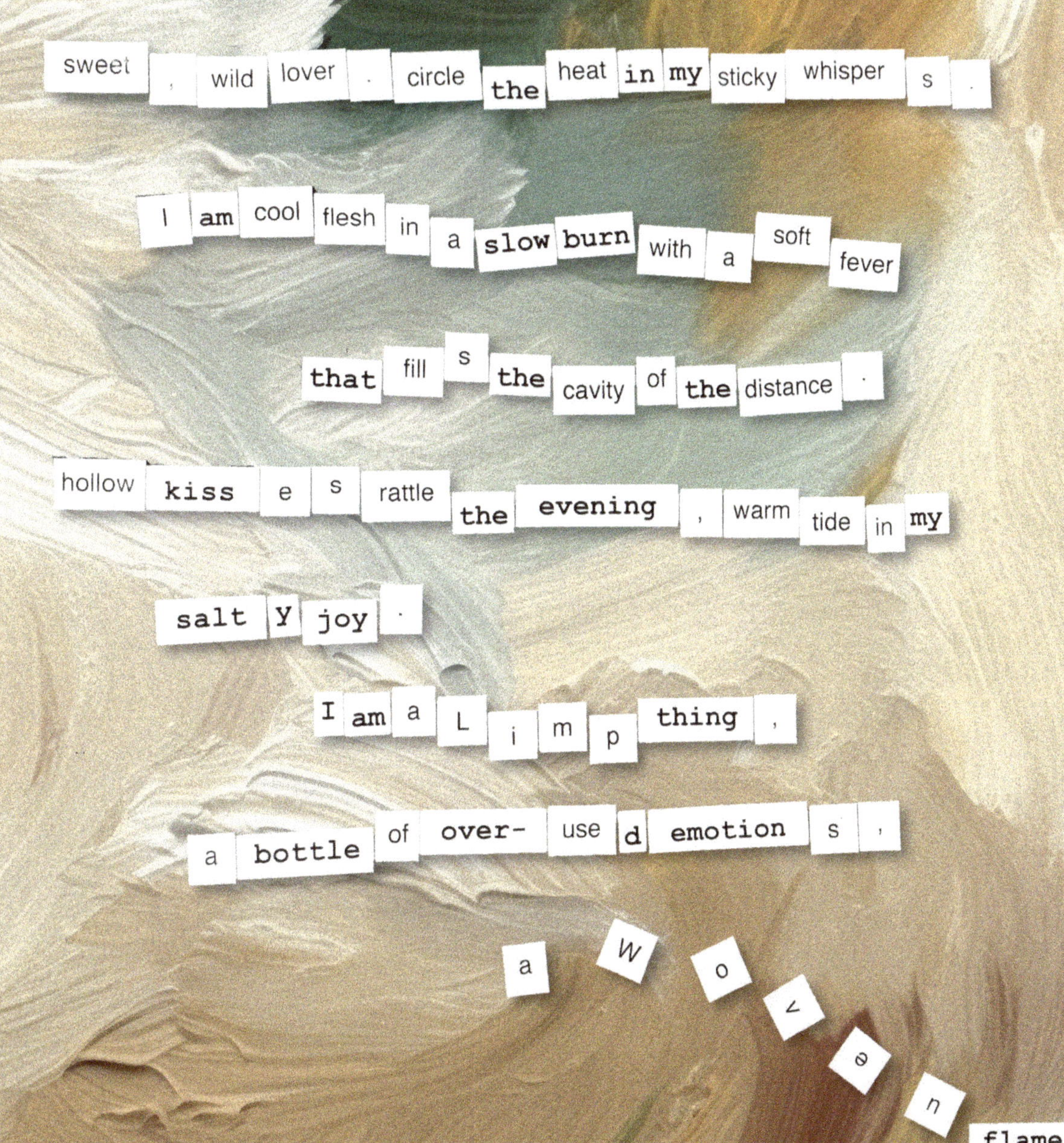

sweet , wild lover . circle the heat in my sticky whisper s .

I am cool flesh in a slow burn with a soft fever

that fill s the cavity of the distance .

hollow kiss e s rattle the evening , warm tide in my

salt y joy .

I am a L i m p thing ,

a bottle of over- use d emotion s ,

a w o v e n flame .

a thirsty sun falls
loose against my
Thin shape, like silk slipping
recklessly through the hands
of a lover
too caught up.
September makes a mess of me with her
sloppy beauty,
all sunburn Thair, full body tease, &
orange romance.

the night is loud with long inhales,
she mourns her modesty, and
I drink her moonlight slow.
a symphony of warm light, a pretty face.
she is earth-shattering,
& I am flat.

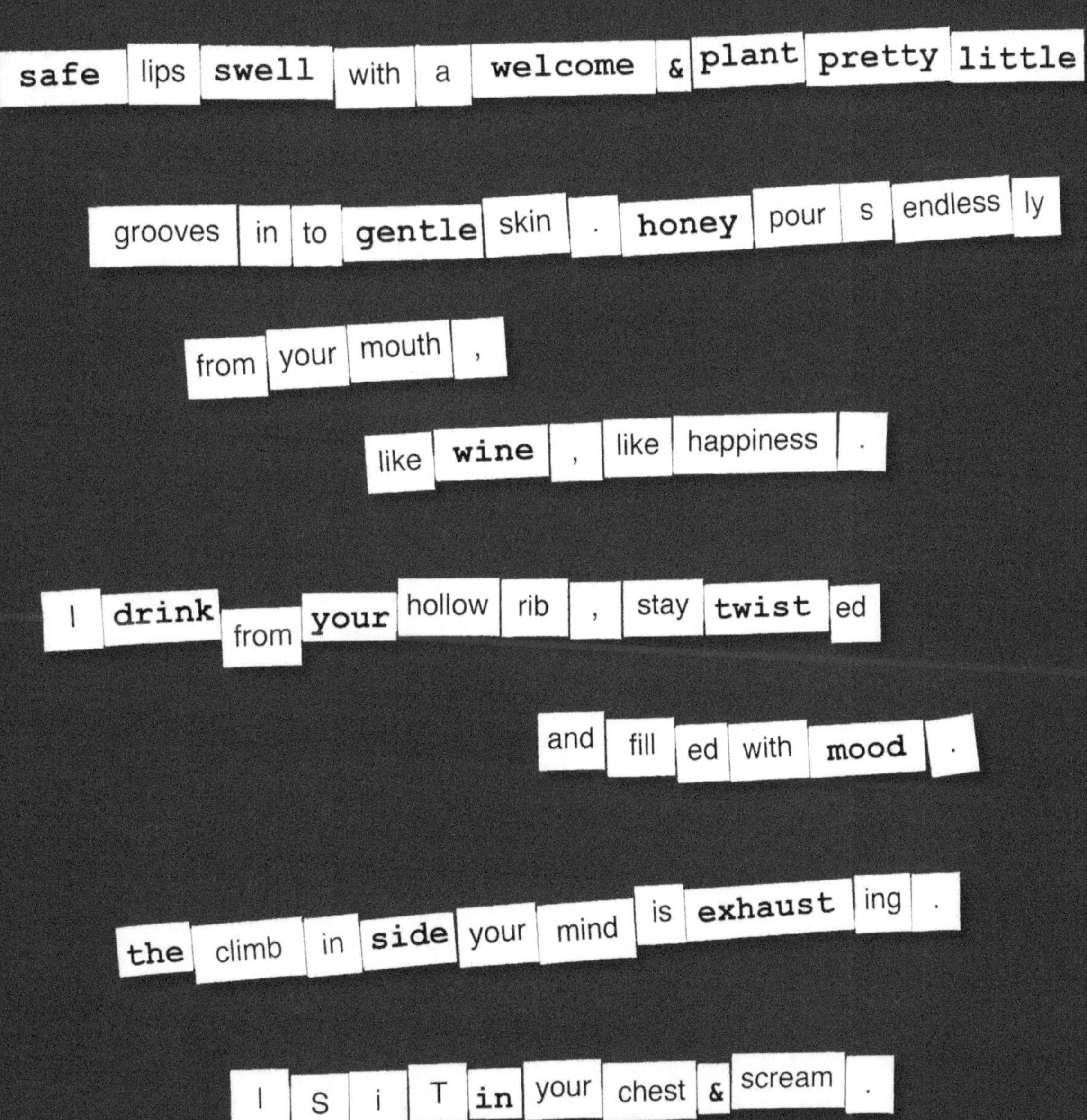

safe lips swell with a welcome & plant pretty little
grooves in to gentle skin . honey pour s endless ly
from your mouth ,
like wine , like happiness .
I drink from your hollow rib , stay twist ed
and fill ed with mood .
the climb in side your mind is exhaust ing .
I S i T in your chest & scream .

lazy is the first look , the secret s that pollinate my cheek .

a lover shape s her mouth to bite an arrow

& I tremble under her r e l e a s e .

lazy is the hollow night , a tasteless world , a stupid need .

lazy is the naked dream , the long shiver ,

the shadow under your laugh .

lazy is the pour ing sunshine , the give easy eyes ,

beautiful beholder er gush ing soft ly .

I felt

, jingle snort s

go

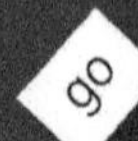

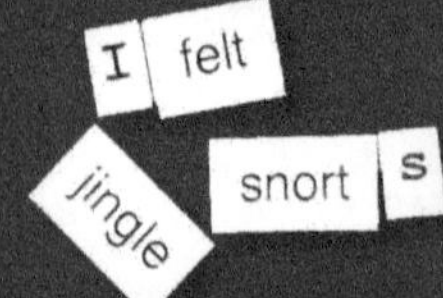

how to say my name

like gossip stick ing on empty breath , like slander .

like when you swallow the failure of a man .

s a y it wrong , be feisty , eight mimosa s deep .

fill your teeth with mud , let Spring bloom & die in your throat .

s a y it loud & blush , smooch it under schoolgirl s skirt s .

like s u n n y side up egg s , morning birth ,

the swell ing of anything bare .

like salt in a w o u n d or

like the triumph of a girl or

like a hollow September .

here are my grooves . my ache to be something soft ,

thick , all consum ing , a Squishee squish .

to belong to two brown eye s .

h e r e are my big feel ing s , my summer heart .

suck the hour s from the sky .

h e r e is my courage to eat , savor the grief ,

turn a shade of blush that is modern . we nest quiet ly .

h e r e is my rumble , my feisty slip of the hand ,

my swollen trust .

h e r E is my bloom , my comfort , the need to cling ,

to twist , to fly inside your mouth .

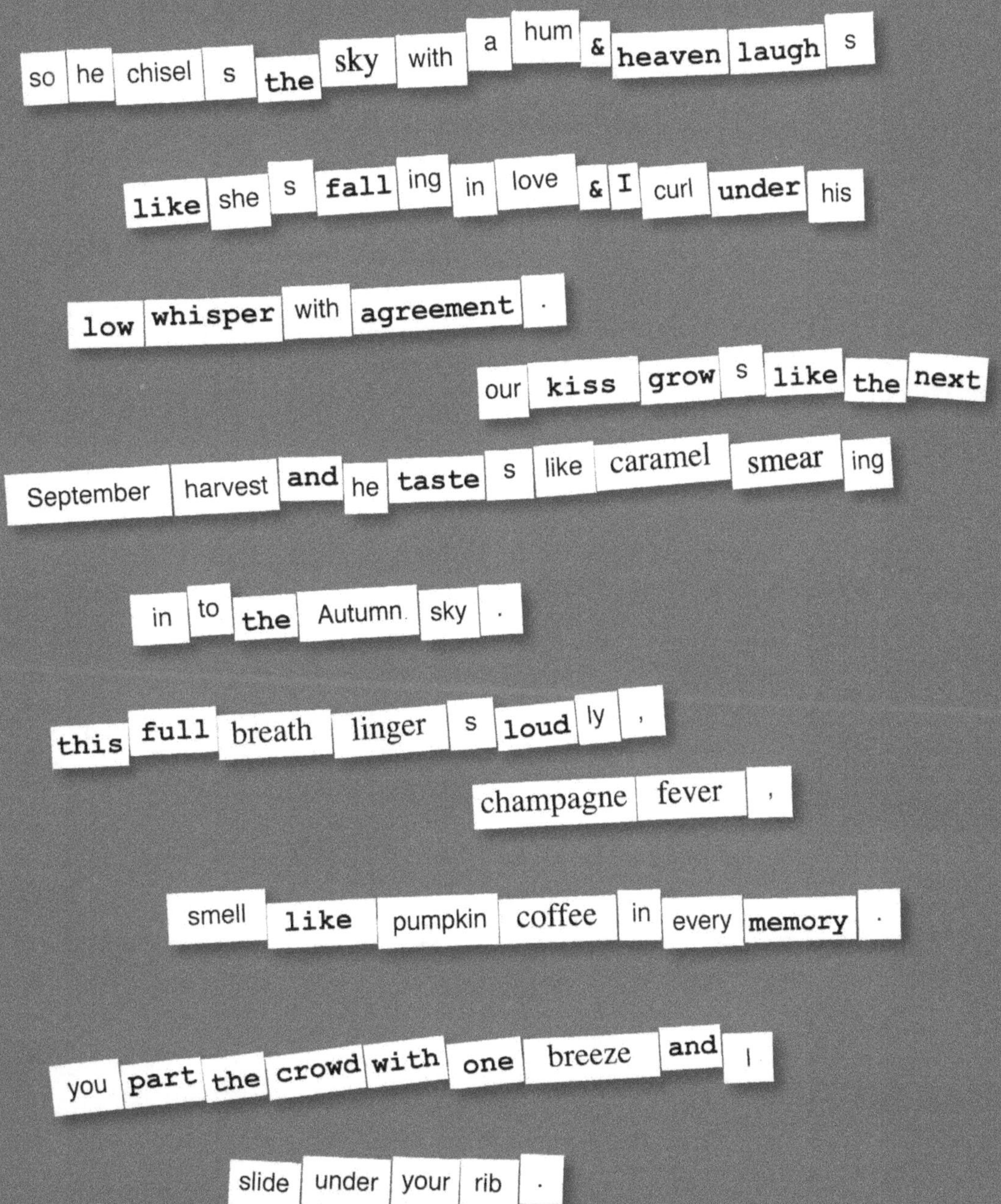

so he chisel s the sky with a hum & heaven laugh s
like she s fall ing in love & I curl under his
low whisper with agreement .
our kiss grow s like the next
September harvest and he taste s like caramel smear ing
in to the Autumn. sky .
this full breath linger s loud ly ,
champagne fever ,
smell like pumpkin coffee in every memory .
you part the crowd with one breeze and I
slide under your rib .

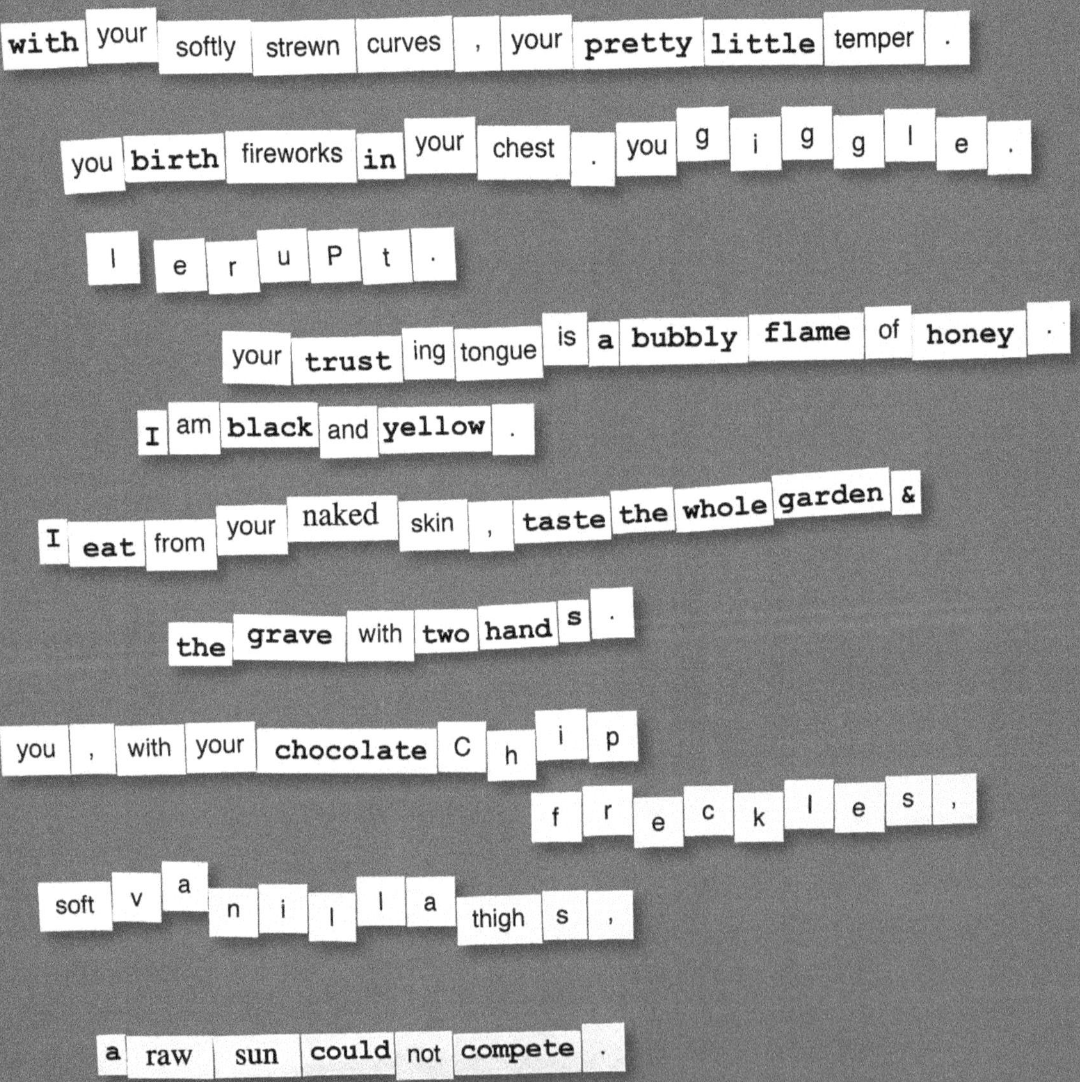

hello beautiful

with your softly strewn curves , your pretty little temper .

you birth fireworks in your chest . you g i g g l e .

I e r u P t .

your trust ing tongue is a bubbly flame of honey .

I am black and yellow .

I eat from your naked skin , taste the whole garden &

the grave with two hand s .

you , with your chocolate C h i p

f r e c k l e s ,

soft v a n i l l a thigh s ,

a raw sun could not compete .

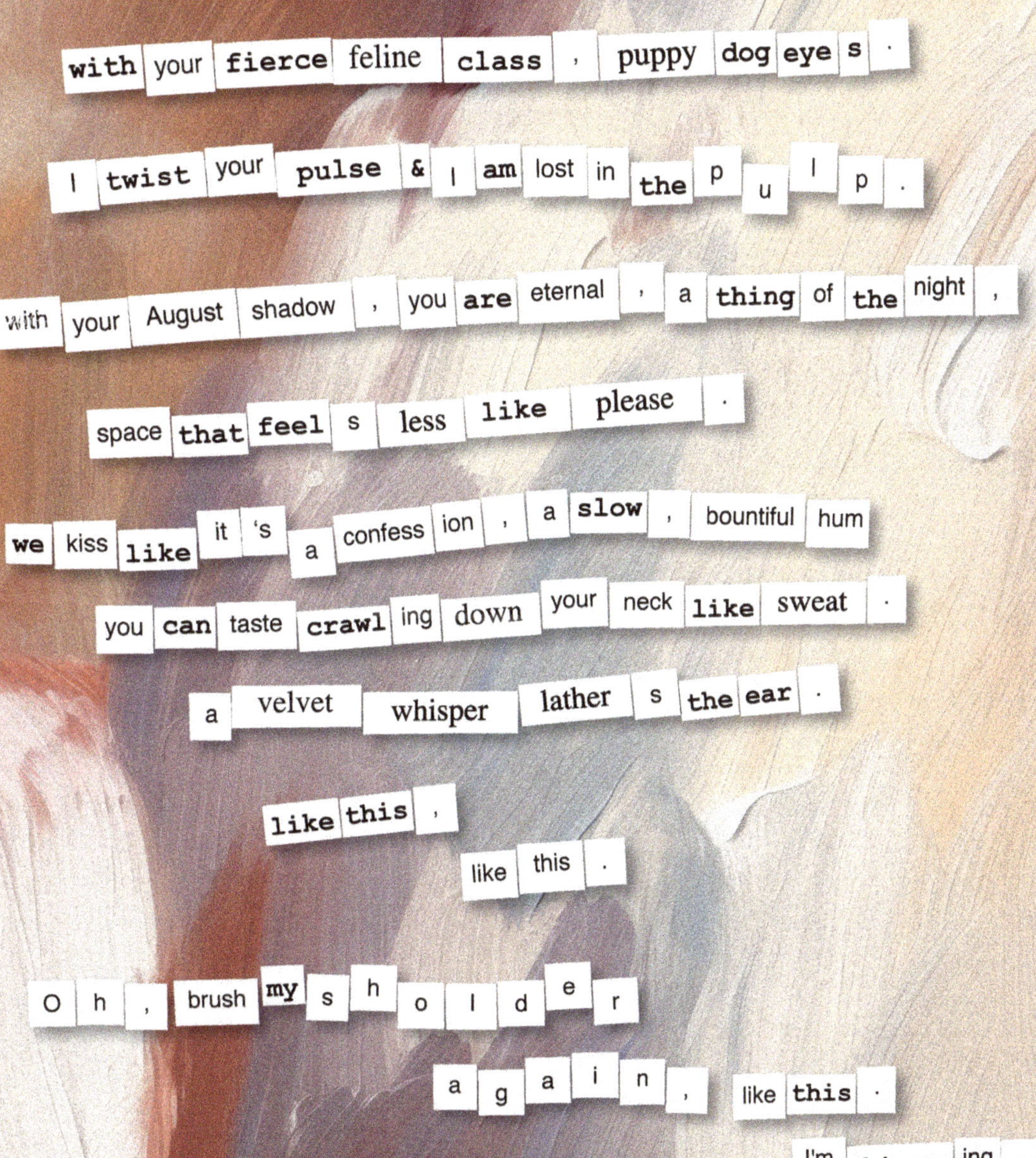

hello beautiful

with your fierce feline class , puppy dog eye s .

I twist your pulse & I am lost in the p u l p .

with your August shadow , you are eternal , a thing of the night ,

space that feel s less like please .

we kiss like it 's a confess ion , a slow , bountiful hum

you can taste crawl ing down your neck like sweat .

a velvet whisper lather s the ear .

like this ,

like this .

Oh , brush my s h o l d e r

a g a i n , like this .

I'm shiver ing .

Weird girl

a chick with **ceiling grief** , raisin **eye** s , drink s
from **high heels** , **a pamper** ed **wreck** .

a petal that broke , a pumpkin pleas er , **juicy heart**
linger er , **flibbertigibbets girl** .
enthusiastic about boob s , **a thirsty** ape ,

a child within a **wine** garden , a teas ing **savage** with
bonfire hair , **a proper thank** you girl .

a girl with **birth** in her hip s & a peach **y personality** ,
an **intoxicate** d appetite , summer lick s her neck .

weird girl ,

schoolgirl ,

good **girl** ,

relax , **girl** .

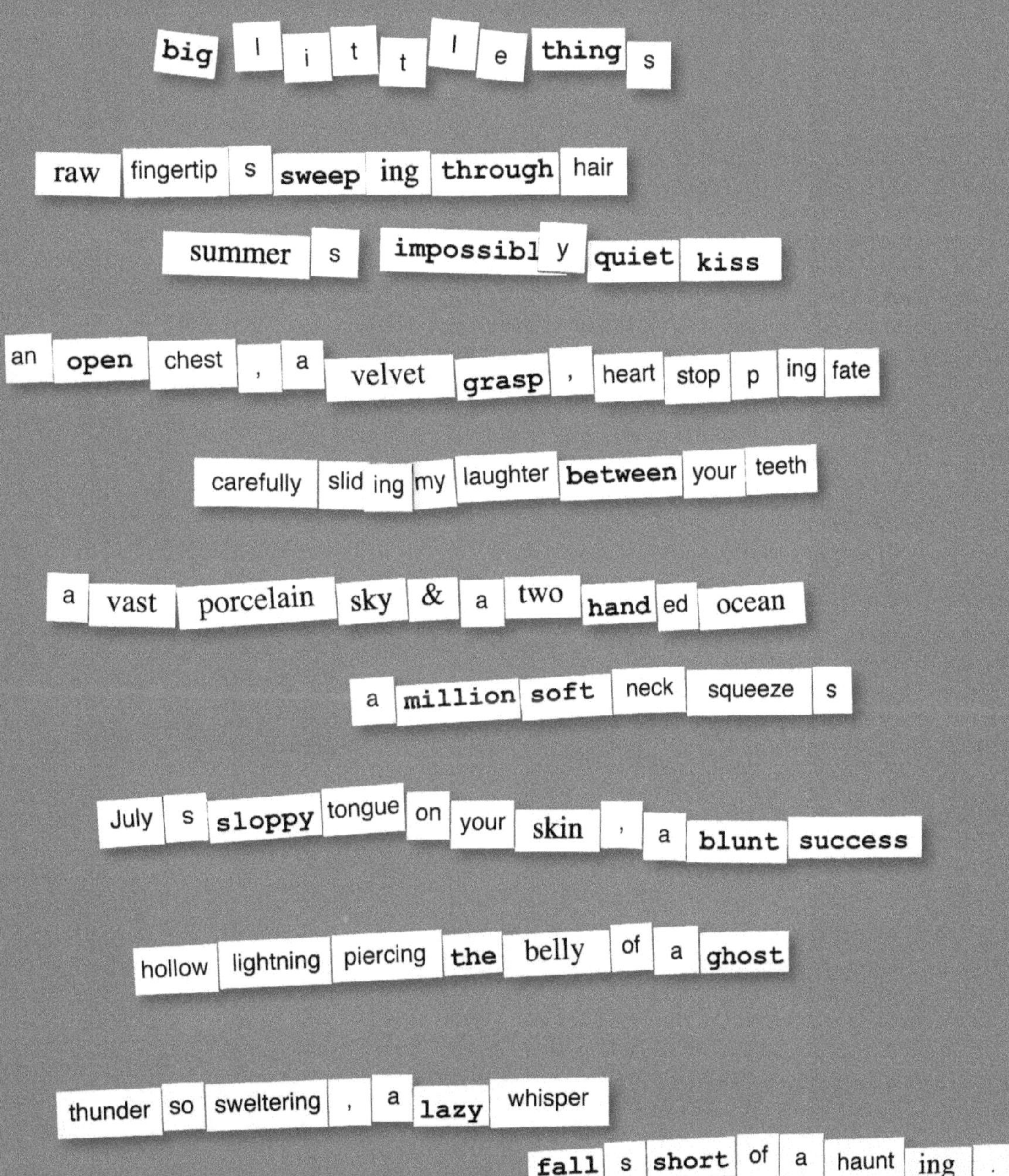

big little things
raw fingertip s sweep ing through hair
summer s impossibl y quiet kiss
an open chest , a velvet grasp , heart stop p ing fate
carefully slid ing my laughter between your teeth
a vast porcelain sky & a two hand ed ocean
a million soft neck squeeze s
July s sloppy tongue on your skin , a blunt success
hollow lightning piercing the belly of a ghost
thunder so sweltering , a lazy whisper
fall s short of a haunt ing .

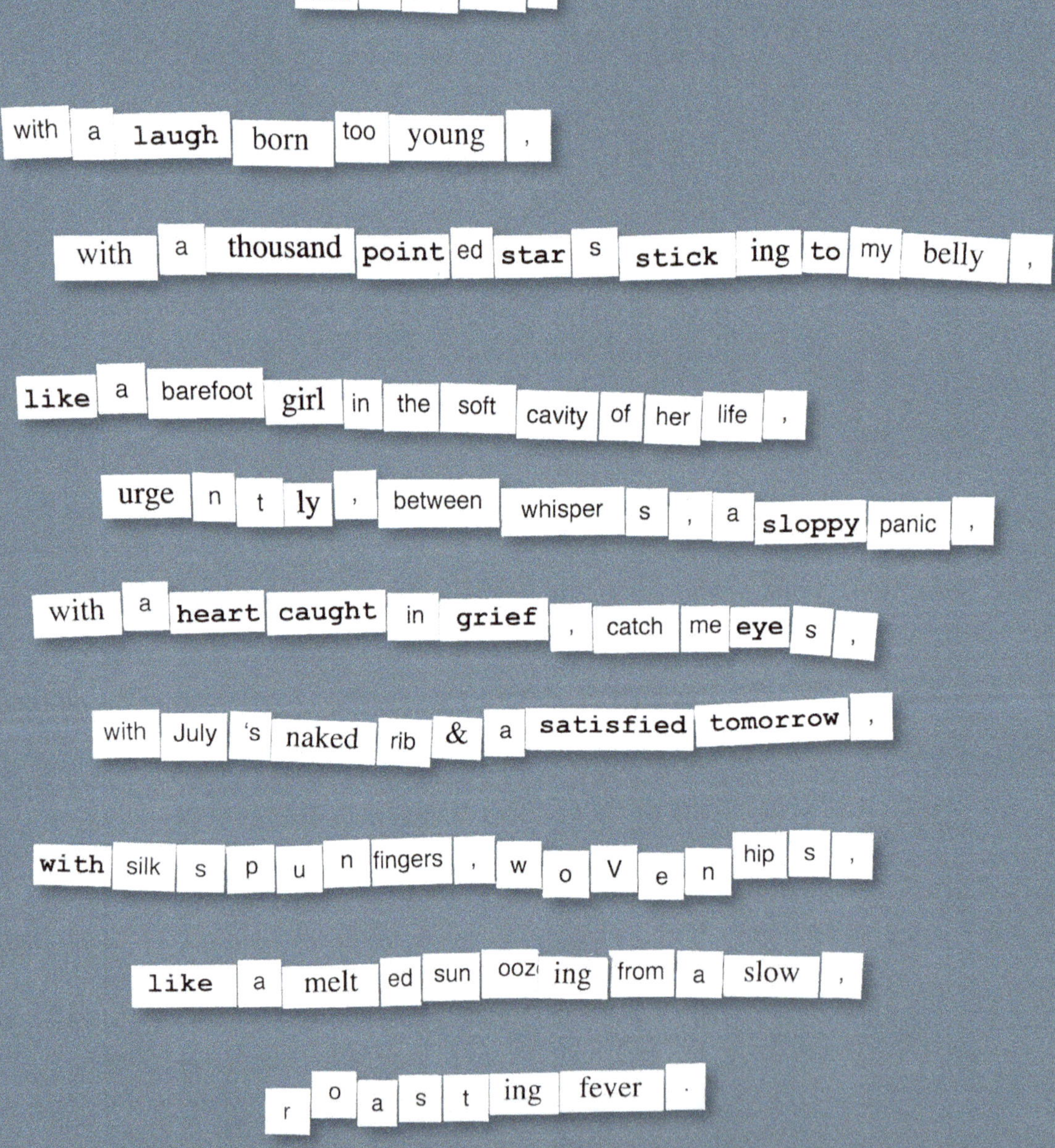

how do you love ?

with a laugh born too young ,

with a thousand pointed stars sticking to my belly ,

like a barefoot girl in the soft cavity of her life ,

urgently , between whispers , a sloppy panic ,

with a heart caught in grief , catch me eyes ,

with July 's naked rib & a satisfied tomorrow ,

with silk spun fingers , woven hips ,

like a melted sun oozing from a slow ,

roasting fever .

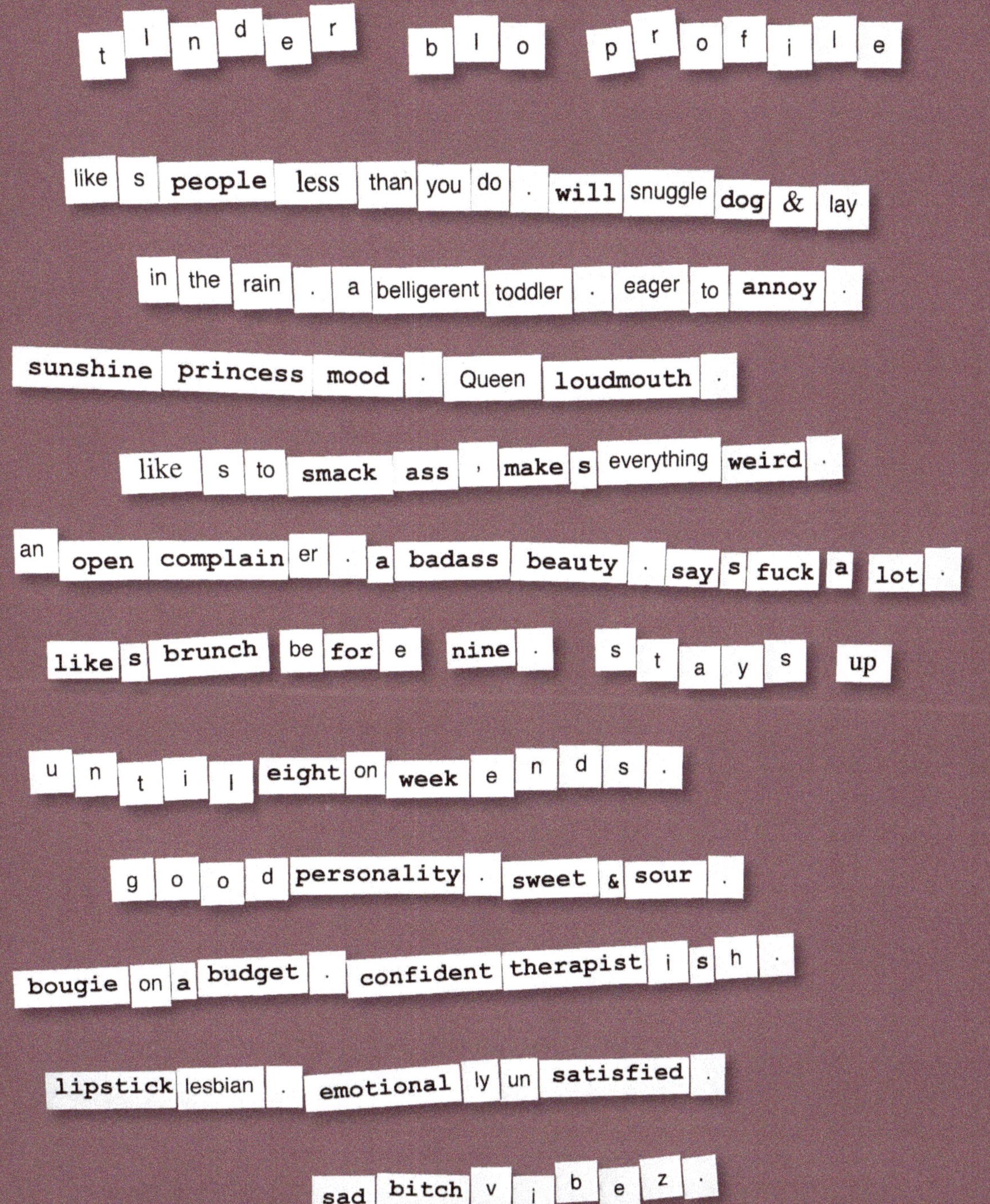

tinder blo profile

likes people less than you do . will snuggle dog & lay
in the rain . a belligerent toddler . eager to annoy .
sunshine princess mood . Queen loudmouth .
likes to smack ass , makes everything weird .
an open complainer . a badass beauty . says fuck a lot .
likes brunch before nine . stays up
until eight on weekends .
good personality . sweet & sour .
bougie on a budget . confident therapist ish .
lipstick lesbian . emotionally unsatisfied .
sad bitch vibez .

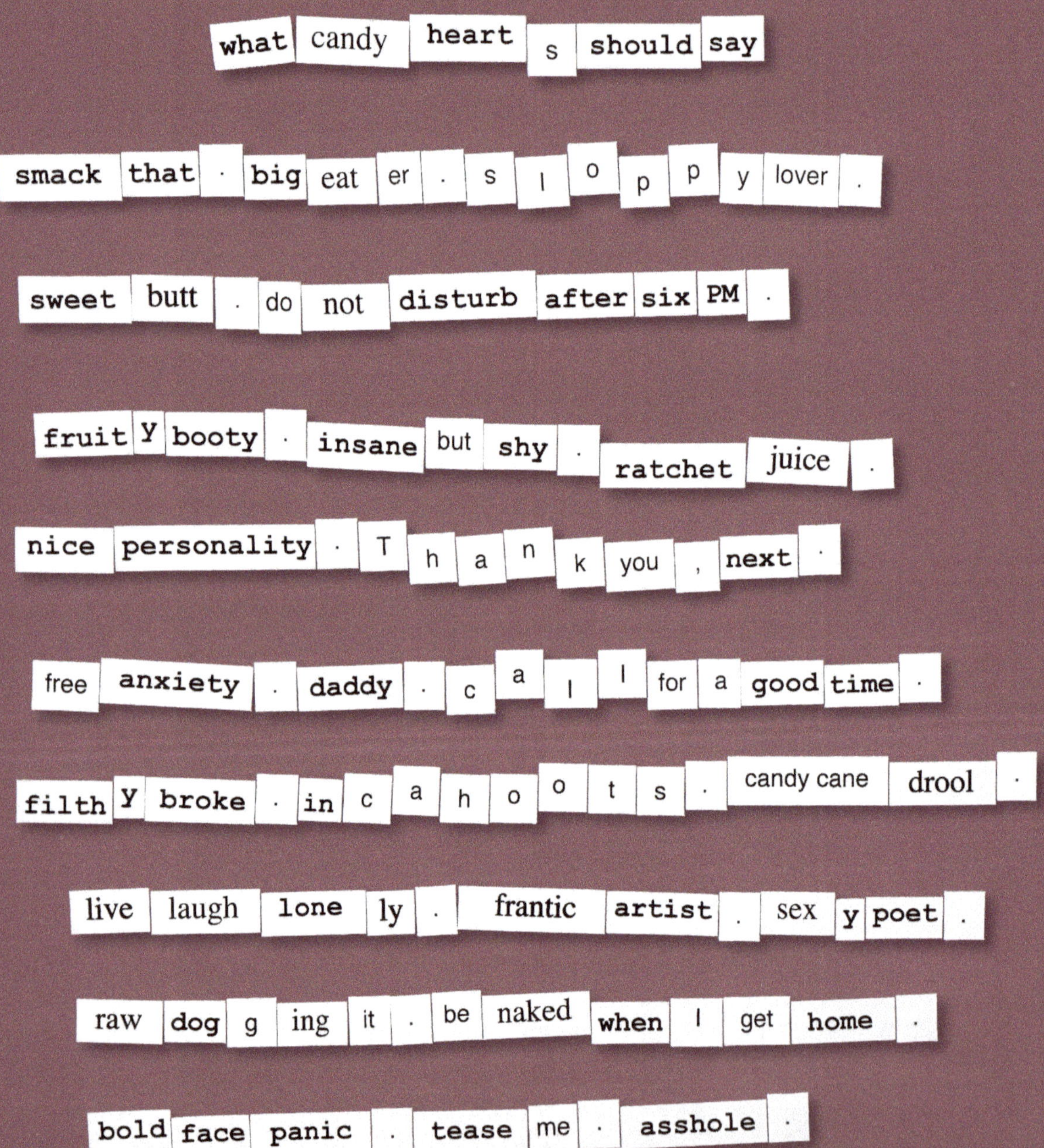

what candy heart s should say
smack that . big eat er . s l o p p y lover .
sweet butt . do not disturb after six PM .
fruit y booty . insane but shy . ratchet juice .
nice personality . T h a n k you , next .
free anxiety . daddy . c a l l for a good time .
filth y broke . in c a h o o t s . candy cane drool .
live laugh lone ly . frantic artist . sex y poet .
raw dog g ing it . be naked when I get home .
bold face panic . tease me . asshole .

all the thing s my heart has be en

a vodka flame of smoke , a frantic mom ,

a pinch ed n e r v e , close d off ,

a trophy for empty women , a grave d u g too deep ,

impossible at best , flat , laughter attach ed

to a stick , , feminine flesh masculine brain ,

manic panic , a glass of wine , a little tacky ,

a flirt ing rant , a drunk love r , a thousand

see - through fingers , the brave one .

I am so in love with you that

French fashion is jealous of your grandiose galoshes in
the Spring . palm tree s open bare legs for you .

I have a loudmouth about your ass , your laugh ,
your proper mouth . I'd eat fruit from your stomach .

I whisper to the spirit s how shy you are .

clear ly brave and sympathetic . embarrass ing ly hot .

I grow sour with fear if you go . I melt in your
fever , fall in to your weird , cool temper ,

blush for too long , everything is green & pink .

naive & drunk , I am in good

hand s .

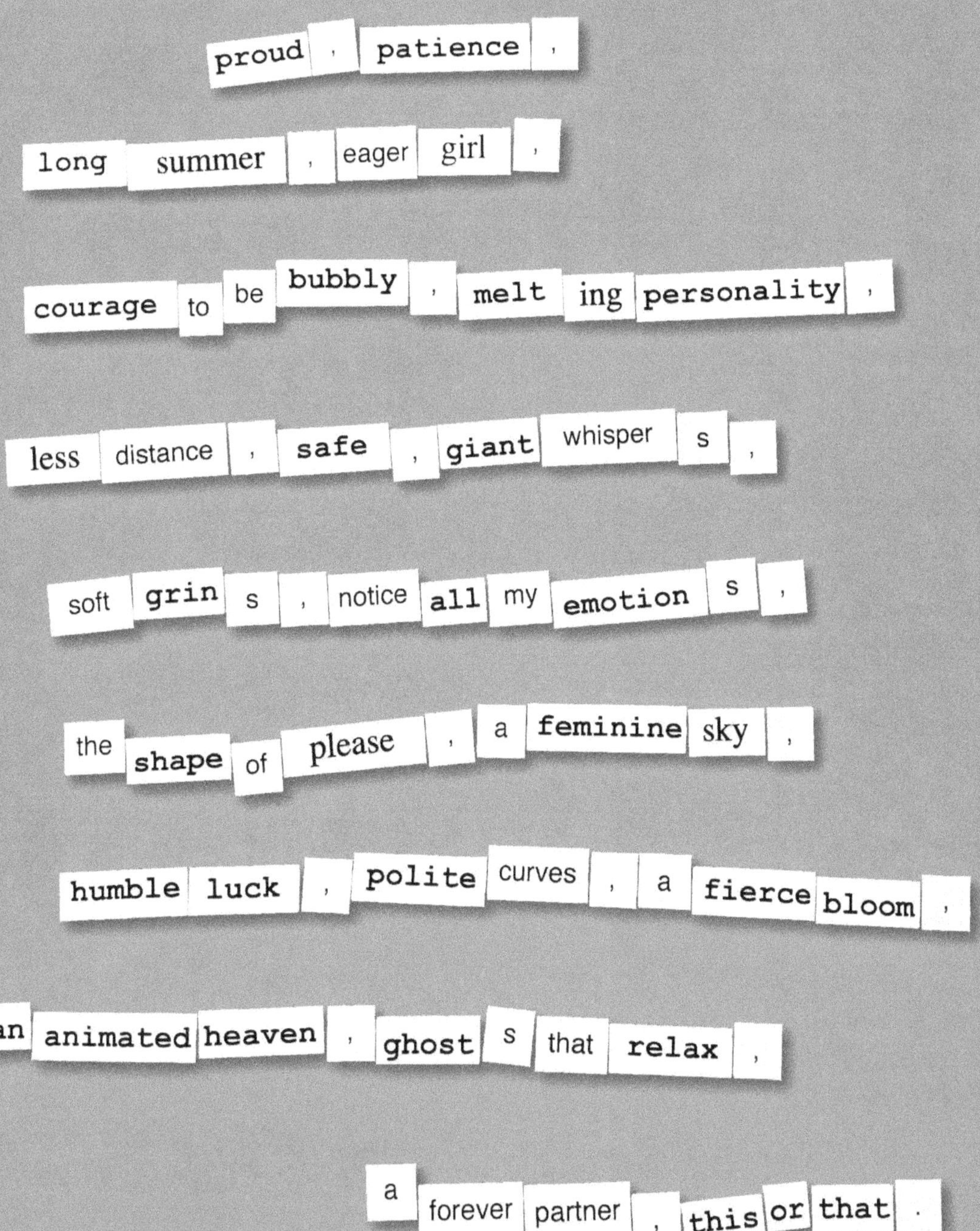
All the words that feel like awh

proud , patience ,

long summer , eager girl ,

courage to be bubbly , melt ing personality ,

less distance , safe , giant whisper s ,

soft grin s , notice all my emotion s ,

the shape of please , a feminine sky ,

humble luck , polite curves , a fierce bloom ,

an animated heaven , ghost s that relax ,

a forever partner , this or that .

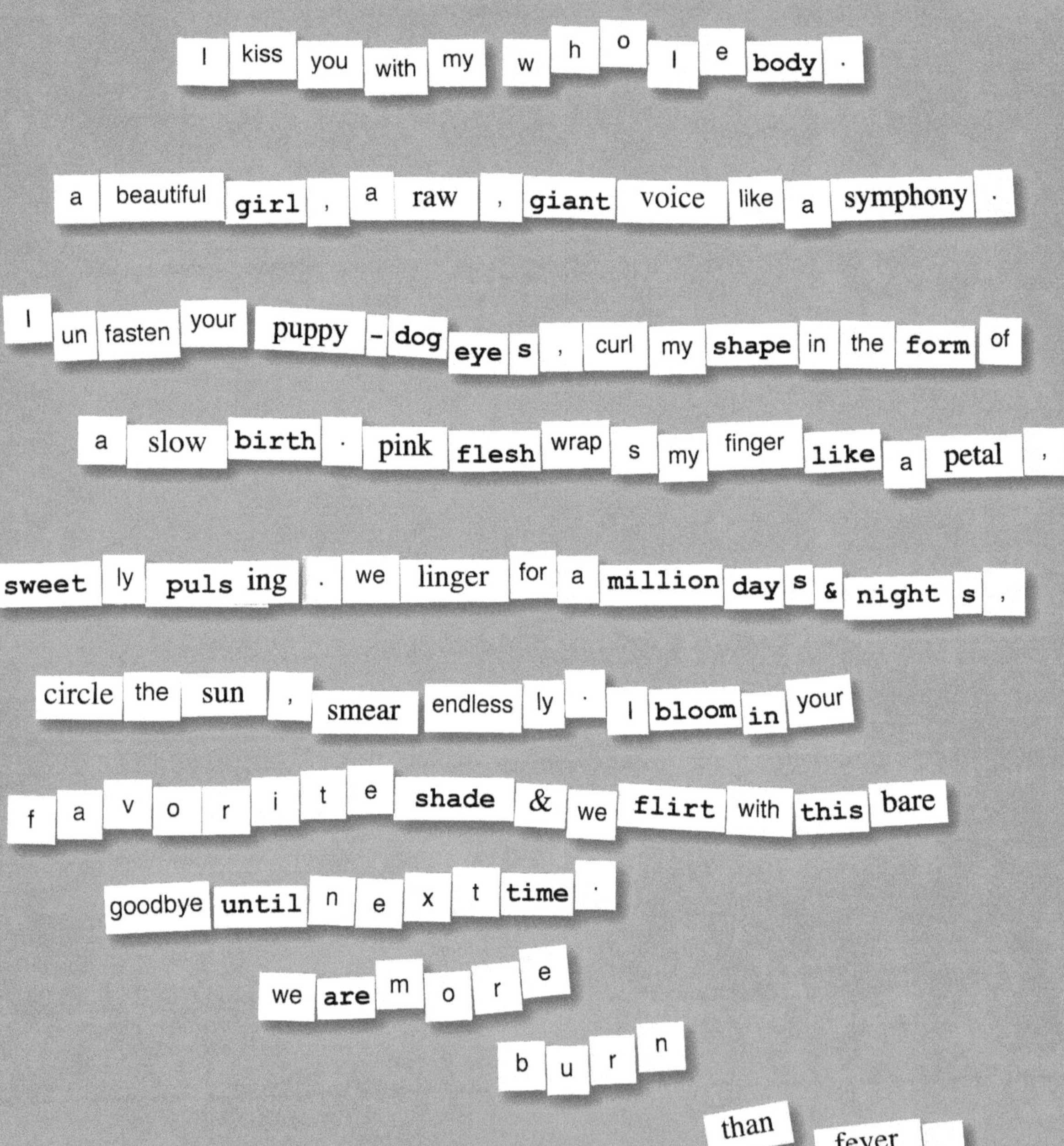

I kiss you with my whole body.
a beautiful girl, a raw, giant voice like a symphony.
I unfasten your puppy-dog eyes, curl my shape in the form of
a slow birth. pink flesh wraps my finger like a petal,
sweetly pulsing. we linger for a million days & nights,
circle the sun, smear endlessly. I bloom in your
favorite shade & we flirt with this bare
goodbye until next time.
we are more
burn
than fever.

54

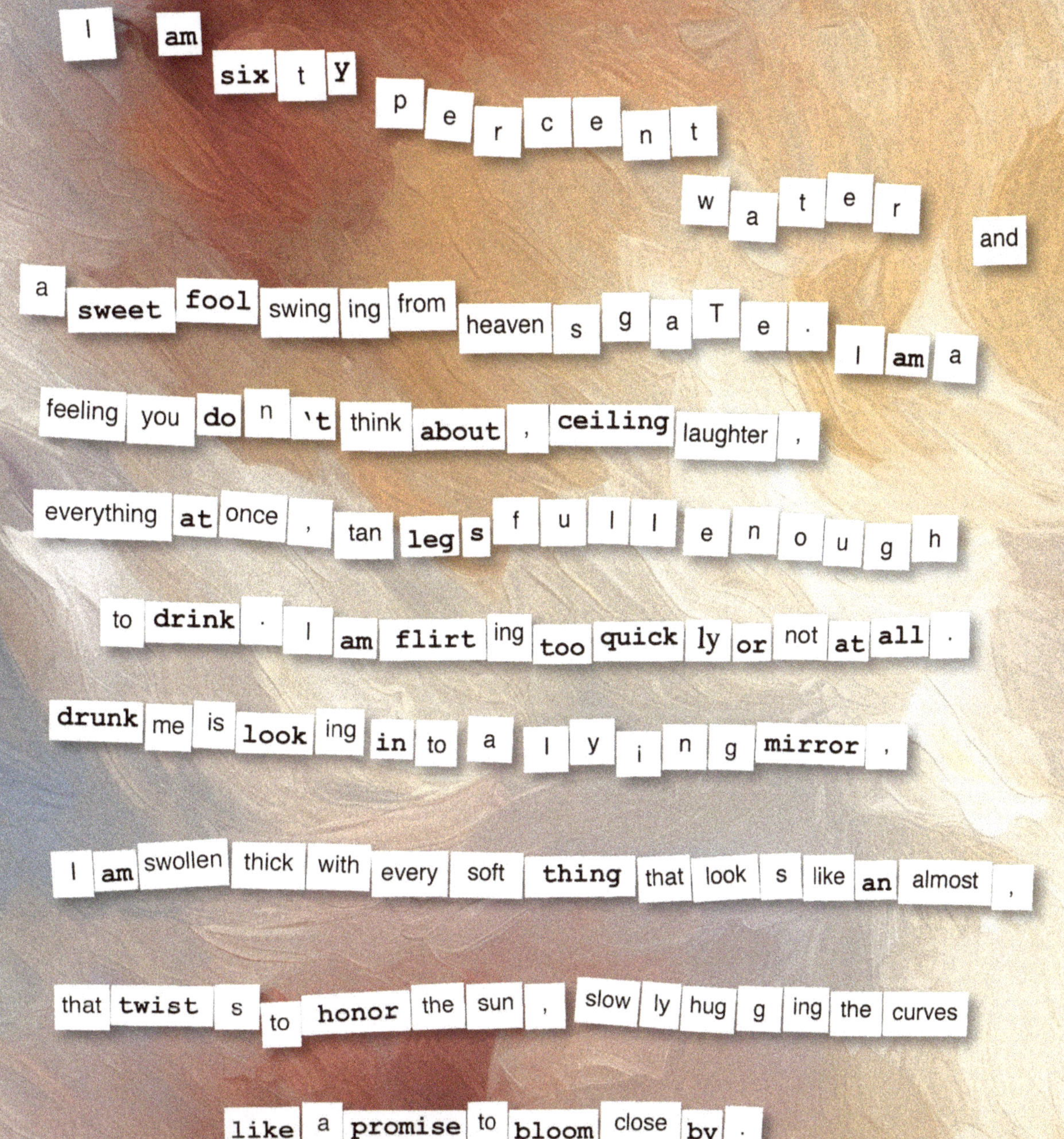

I am sixty percent water and a sweet fool swinging from heavens gaTe. I am a feeling you don't think about, ceiling laughter, everything at once, tan legs full enough to drink. I am flirting too quickly or not at all. drunk me is looking into a lying mirror, I am swollen thick with every soft thing that looks like an almost, that twists to honor the sun, slowly hugging the curves like a promise to bloom close by.

your hair fall s just to your shoulders and it is soft er than my slow curves . I carve your voice from your chest . imagine a life too tall to see over . always ambitious and disappoint ed . we shake the sun of his extra morning fat , keep ing a pinch of swollen sunshine for dinner . my sloppy luck cling s through the whole night , as if I could birth a new belly and make a home for two . everything is too quiet when you kiss me , like a porcelain sky a sleep .

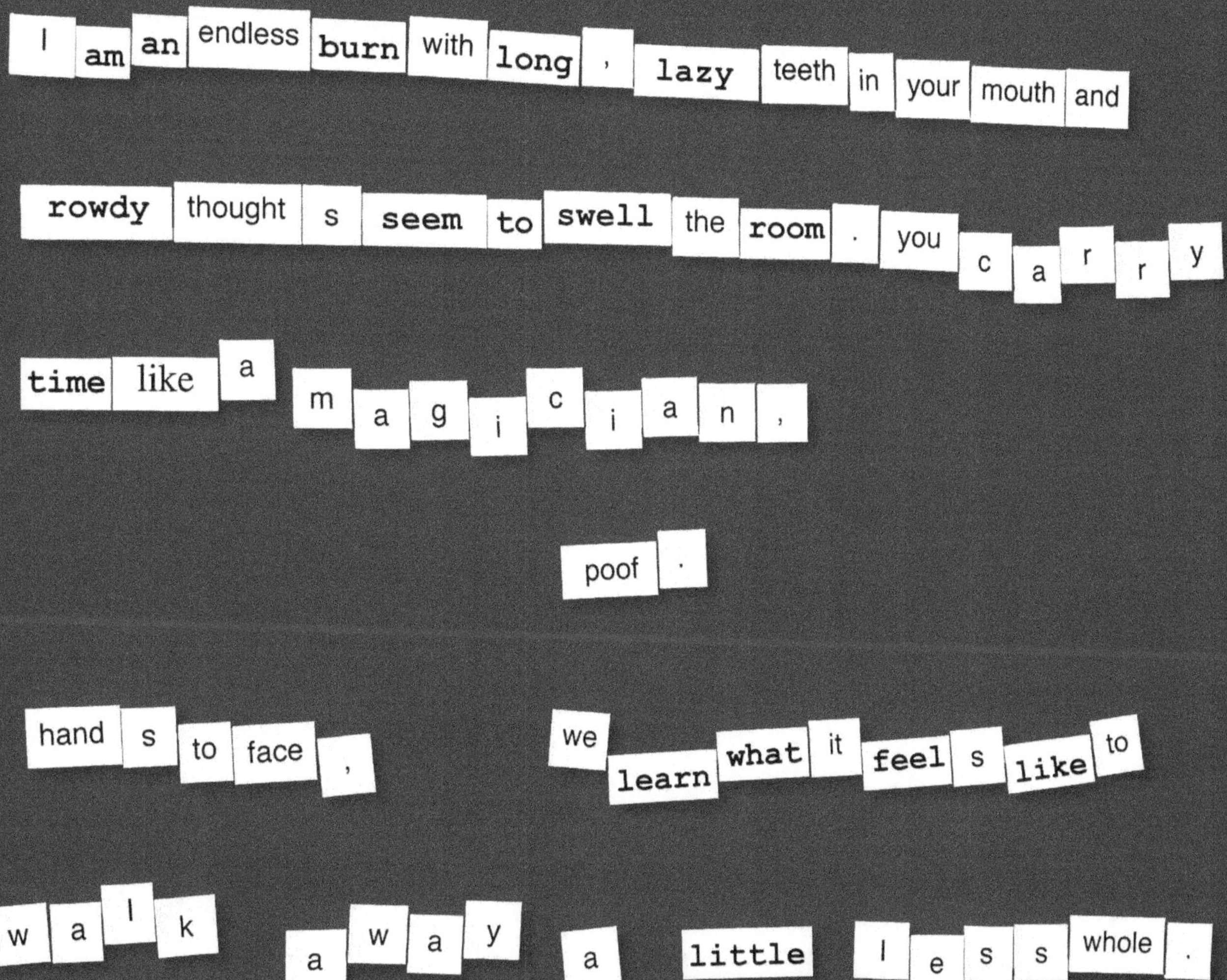

I am an endless burn with long , lazy teeth in your mouth and
rowdy thought s seem to swell the room . you carry
time like a magician ,
poof .
hand s to face , we learn what it feel s like to
walk away a little less whole .

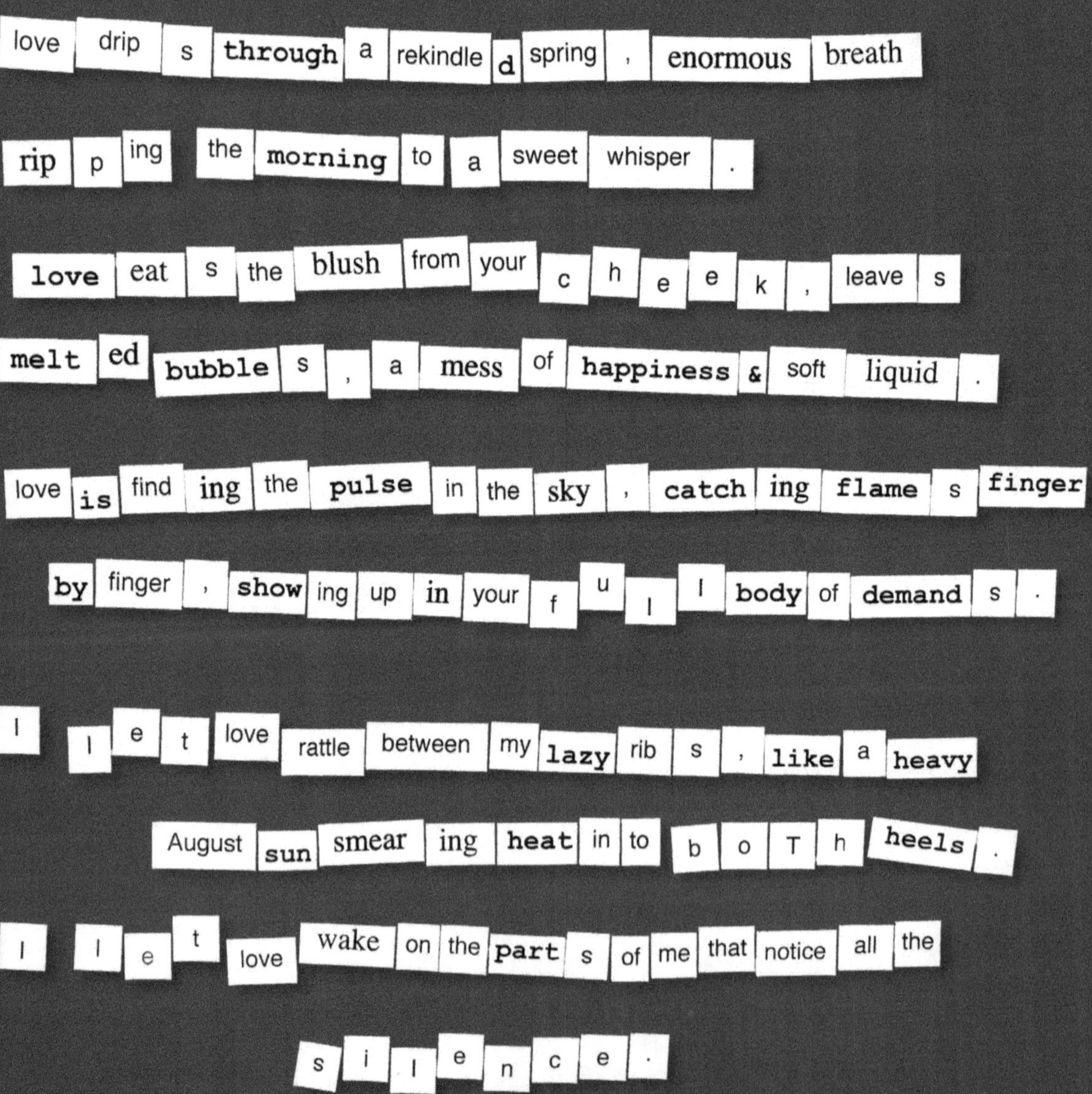

what love I have Left

love drips through a rekindled spring , enormous breath
ripping the morning to a sweet whisper .
love eats the blush from your cheek , leaves
melted bubbles , a mess of happiness & soft liquid .
love is finding the pulse in the sky , catching flames finger
by finger , showing up in your full body of demands .

I let love rattle between my lazy ribs , like a heavy
August sun smearing heat into both heels .
I let love wake on the parts of me that notice all the
silence .

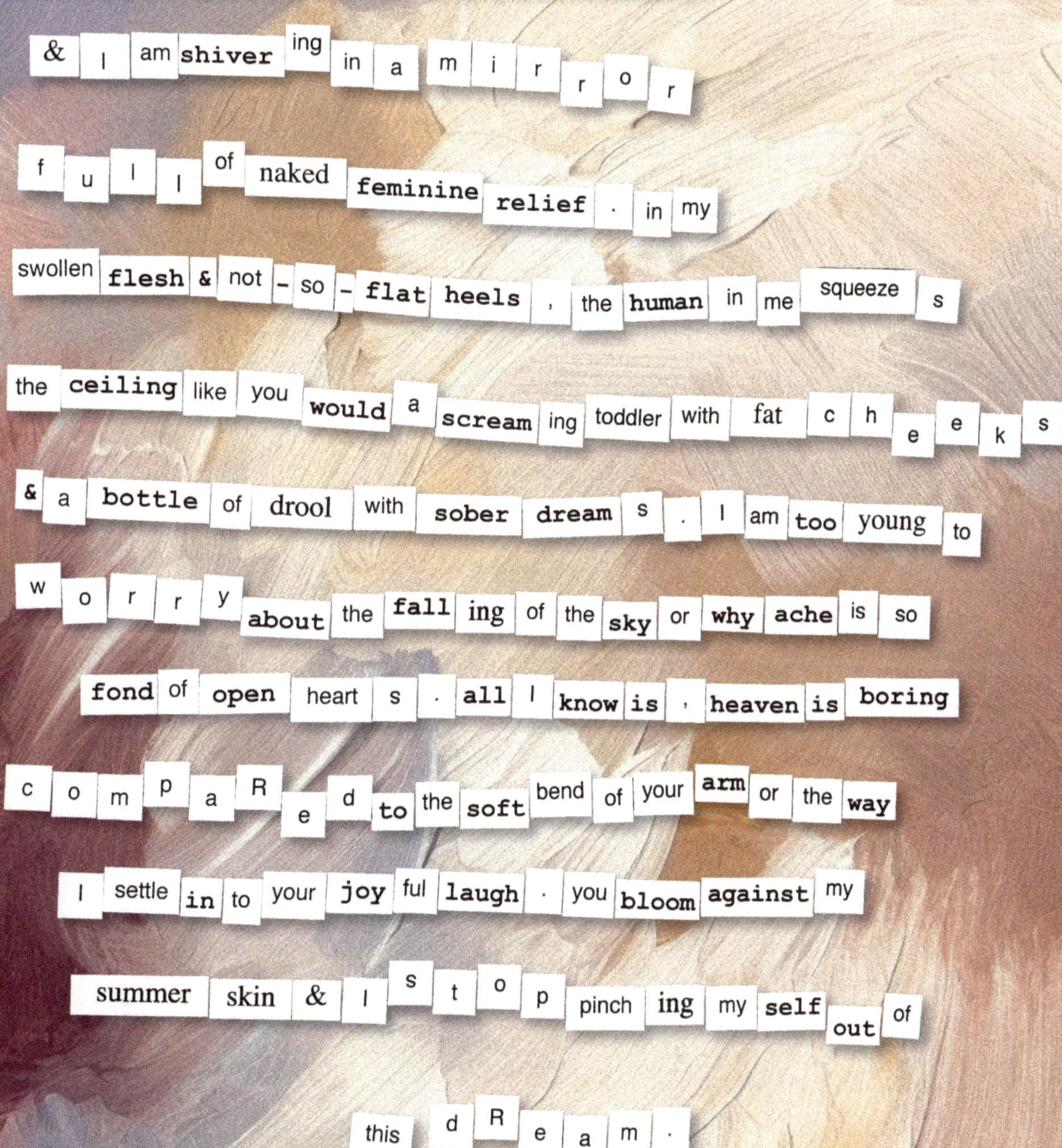

A little lion is snarling at my remote camera

& I am shivering in a mirror

full of naked feminine relief . in my

swollen flesh & not - so - flat heels , the human in me squeezes

the ceiling like you would a screaming toddler with fat cheeks

& a bottle of drool with sober dreams . I am too young to

worry about the falling of the sky or why ache is so

fond of open hearts . all I know is , heaven is boring

compaRed to the soft bend of your arm or the way

I settle into your joyful laugh . you bloom against my

summer skin & I stop pinching myself out of

this dReam .

I'm in my hot girl shit era

I mix a blue & purple outfit, show the mirror my ass,
& dazzle all of walmart with my chill
Vibe. I enjoy my peace, I admire the need to
wreck a naked body, to plunge in to a marvelous glass
of champagne, on that drunk woman shit.

I swear a lot. hell fuck bitch. I'm flat chested
with an enormous heart. grief is a garden I spit up.

I yank flames from my innocent life, complain
about tomorrow, and stab at the sun for being too quiet.

writing poetry is like

pouring love over a reckless idea & waking up

a little sweeter . it is little kisses from life , a birth

you predict . it feels for your hand ,

asks you to dance , it slaps your ass & C alls

you beautiful . it is as big as urgency , a giant belly

thing , & loud like happiness . it is a feast we all stop &

lick on , a body of laughter with enormous wings .

it is soft lipped , full blush , the girl next door .

it is a smooch on the mouth by a gorgeous woman ,

a fierce voice in the night , the breath of a lover .

it is like the first cry of an infants

long life .

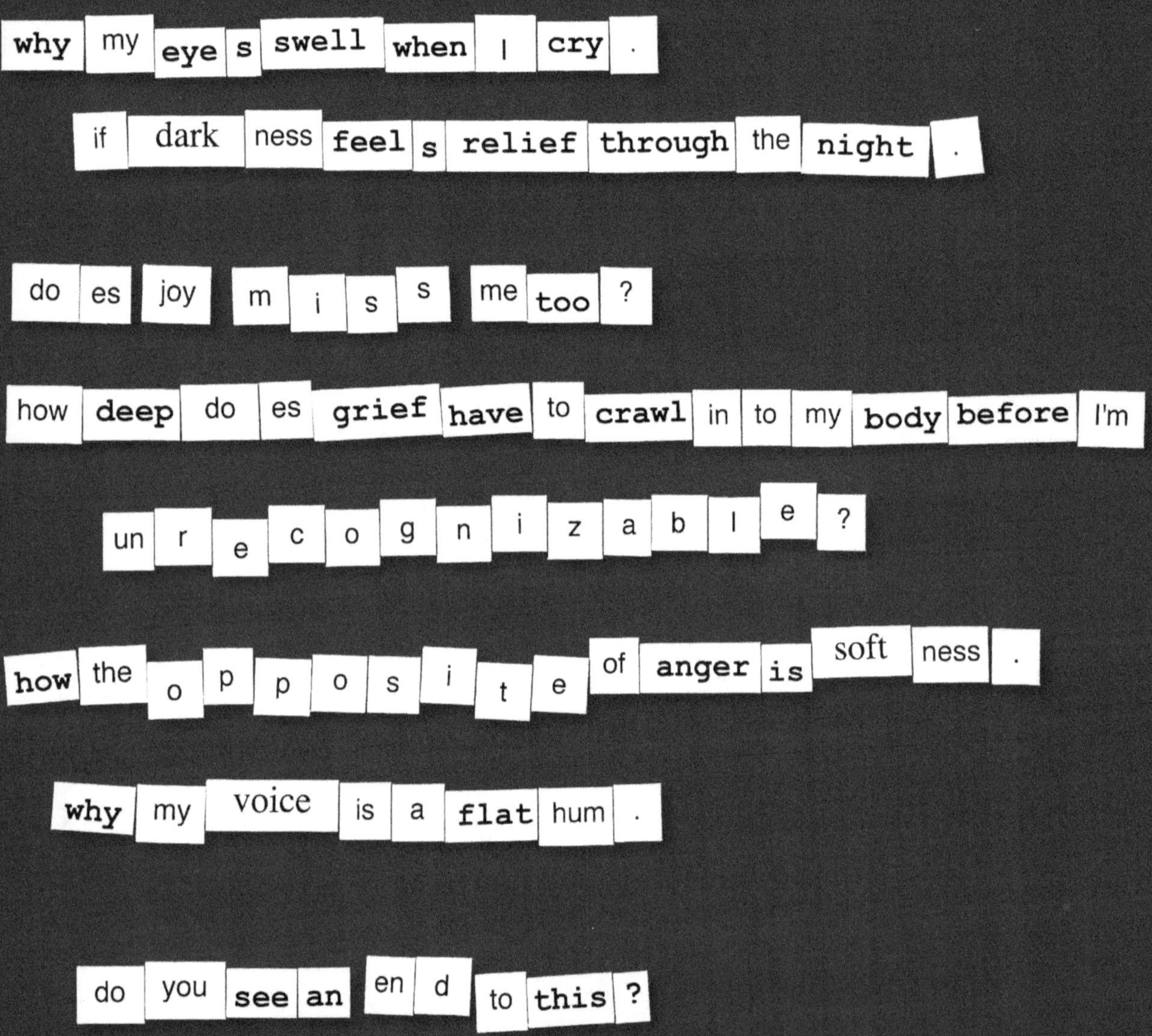

Things I haven't figured out yet

why my eyes swell when I cry .

if darkness feels relief through the night .

does joy miss me too ?

how deep does grief have to crawl into my body before I'm

unrecognizable ?

how the opposite of anger is softness .

why my voice is a flat hum .

do you see an end to this ?

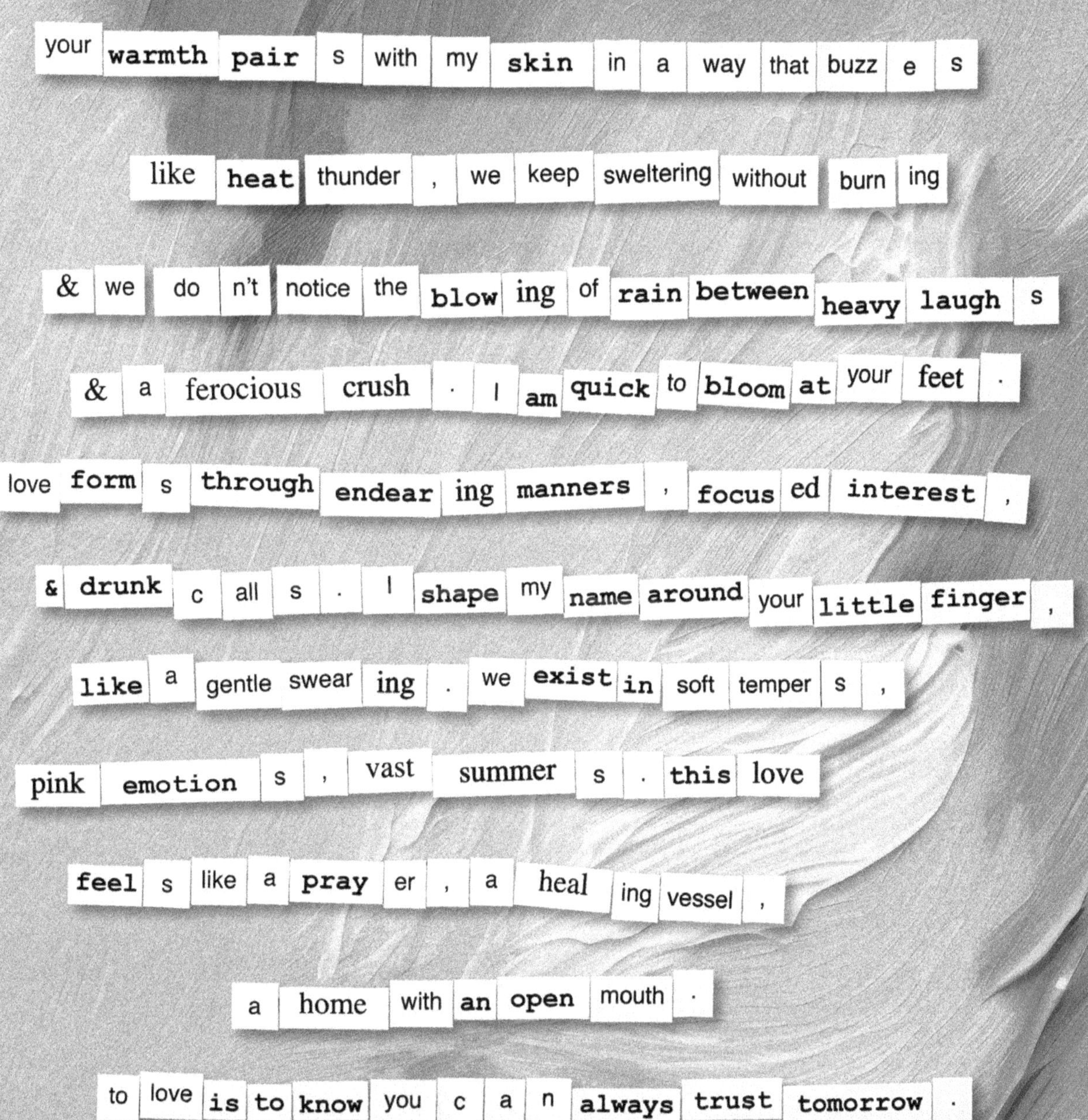

this is love

your warmth pairs with my skin in a way that buzzes

like heat thunder, we keep sweltering without burning

& we don't notice the blowing of rain between heavy laughs

& a ferocious crush. I am quick to bloom at your feet.

love forms through endearing manners, focused interest,

& drunk calls. I shape my name around your little finger,

like a gentle swearing. we exist in soft tempers,

pink emotions, vast summers. this love

feels like a prayer, a healing vessel,

a home with an open mouth.

to love is to know you can always trust tomorrow.

fingertip s like **rain** beneath my **flesh** , I watch effortlessly

as your marble **romance** smear s **in to** a **hot** fever .

like a color ful smile with the taste of honey between **each**

t o o t h , **like** a throat with **an open flame** , like

candy cane **finger** s linger ing **against** a **light** voice .

I smooth your **hair** , **make** an eternity **slow down** , and

feel my swollen breath **whine** · you c all me a **fool** for

this young love , like a **child with** an u r g e n t

shadow · **this storm** in my chest has a **brain**

of it s o w n .

god is a woman

& time is dull & she weep s emotion s

with long , certain relief . a silk

tongue crush es her greed in a smooth

shape . soft , marble light is naked

on her face & I am beneath her with

imperfect s h o e s & an idea of love .

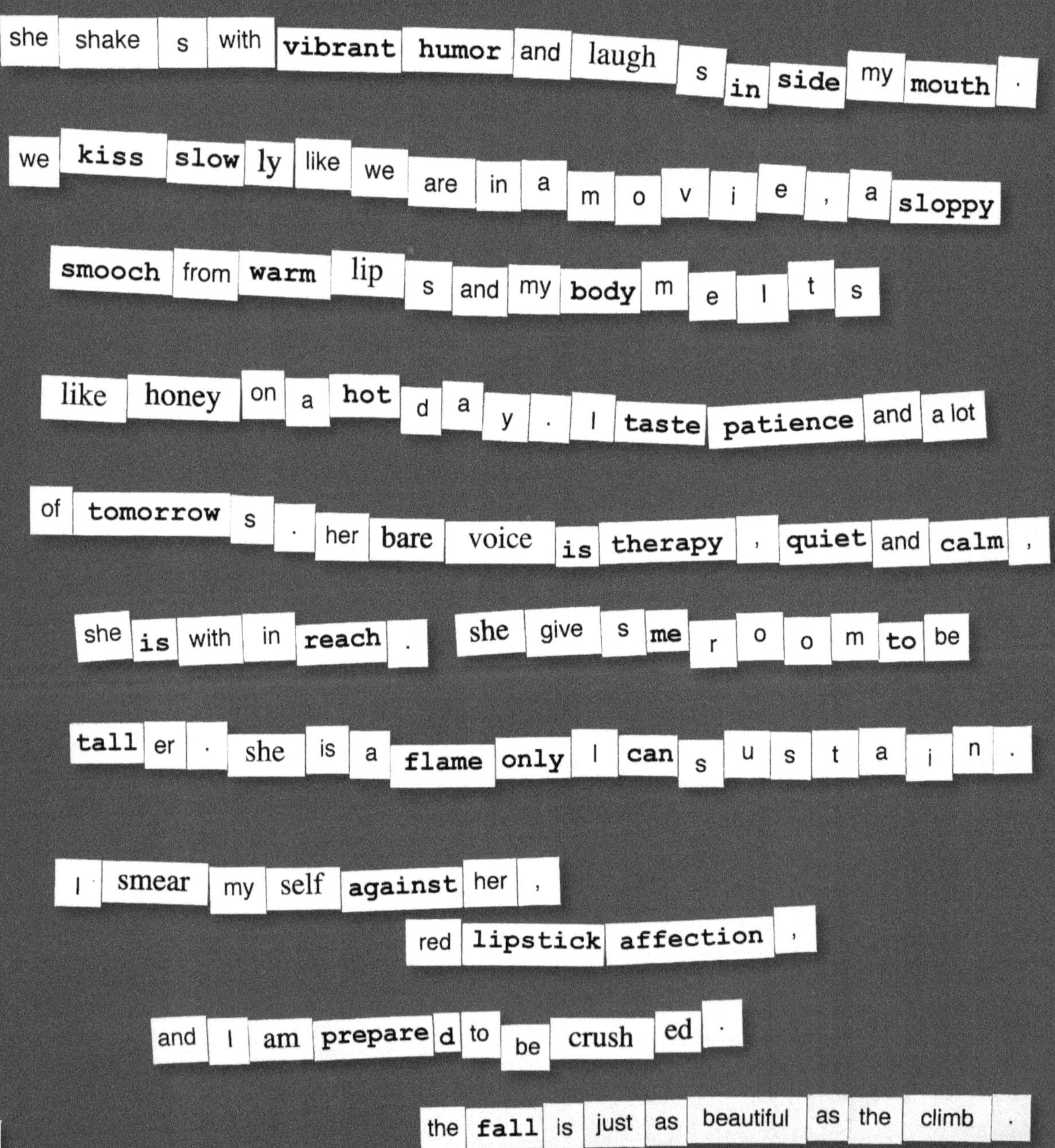

her
she shake s with vibrant humor and laugh s in side my mouth .
we kiss slow ly like we are in a m o v i e , a sloppy
smooch from warm lip s and my body m e l t s
like honey on a hot d a y . I taste patience and a lot
of tomorrow s . her bare voice is therapy , quiet and calm ,
she is with in reach . she give s me r o o m to be
tall er . she is a flame only I can s u s t a i n .
I smear my self against her ,
red lipstick affection ,
and I am prepare d to be crush ed .
the fall is just as beautiful as the climb .

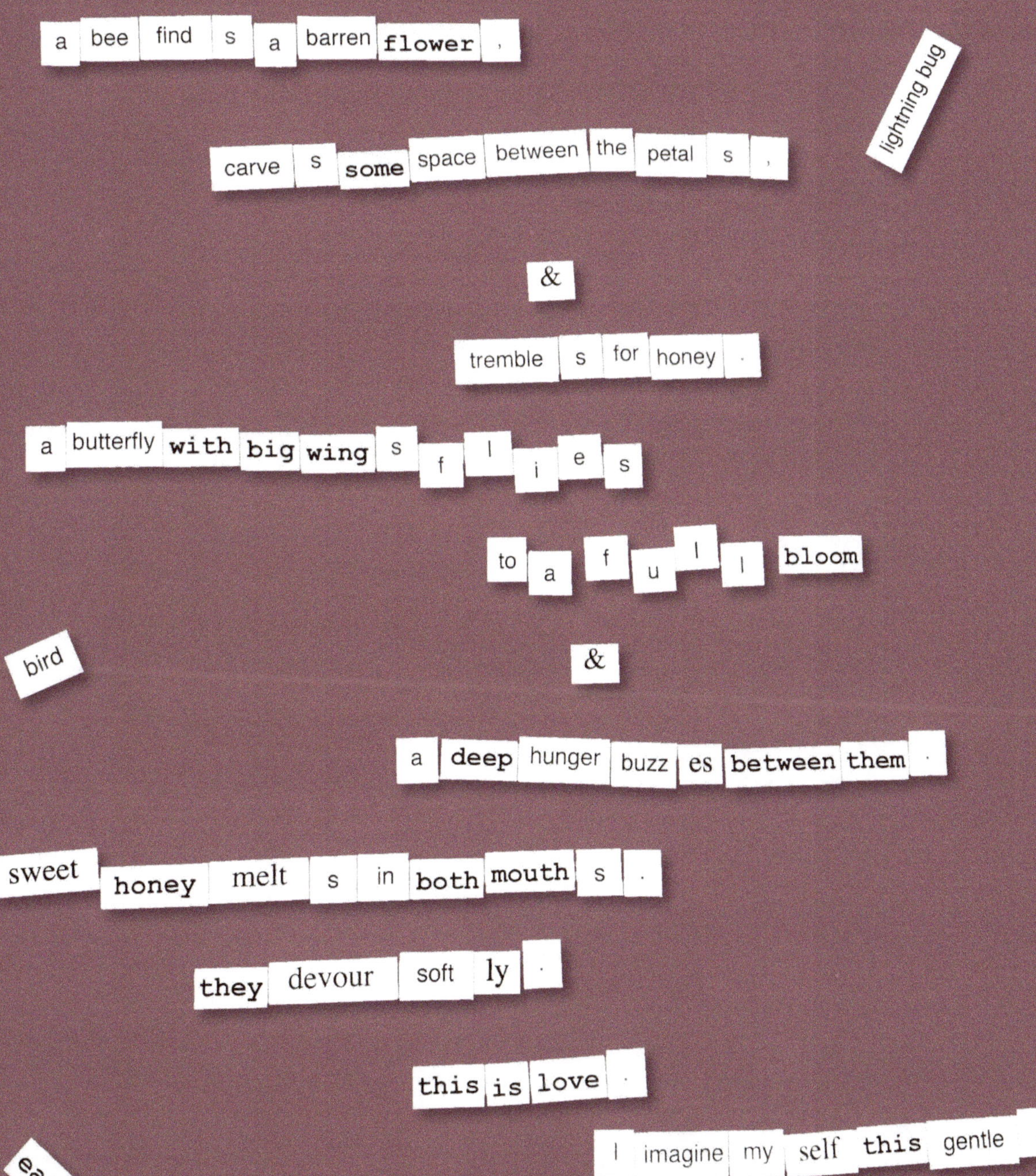

a bee find s a barren flower ,
carve s some space between the petal s ,
lightning bug
&
tremble s for honey .
a butterfly with big wing s f l i e s
to a f u l l bloom
bird
&
a deep hunger buzz es between them .
sweet honey melt s in both mouth s .
they devour soft ly .
this is love .
eat
I imagine my self this gentle .

67

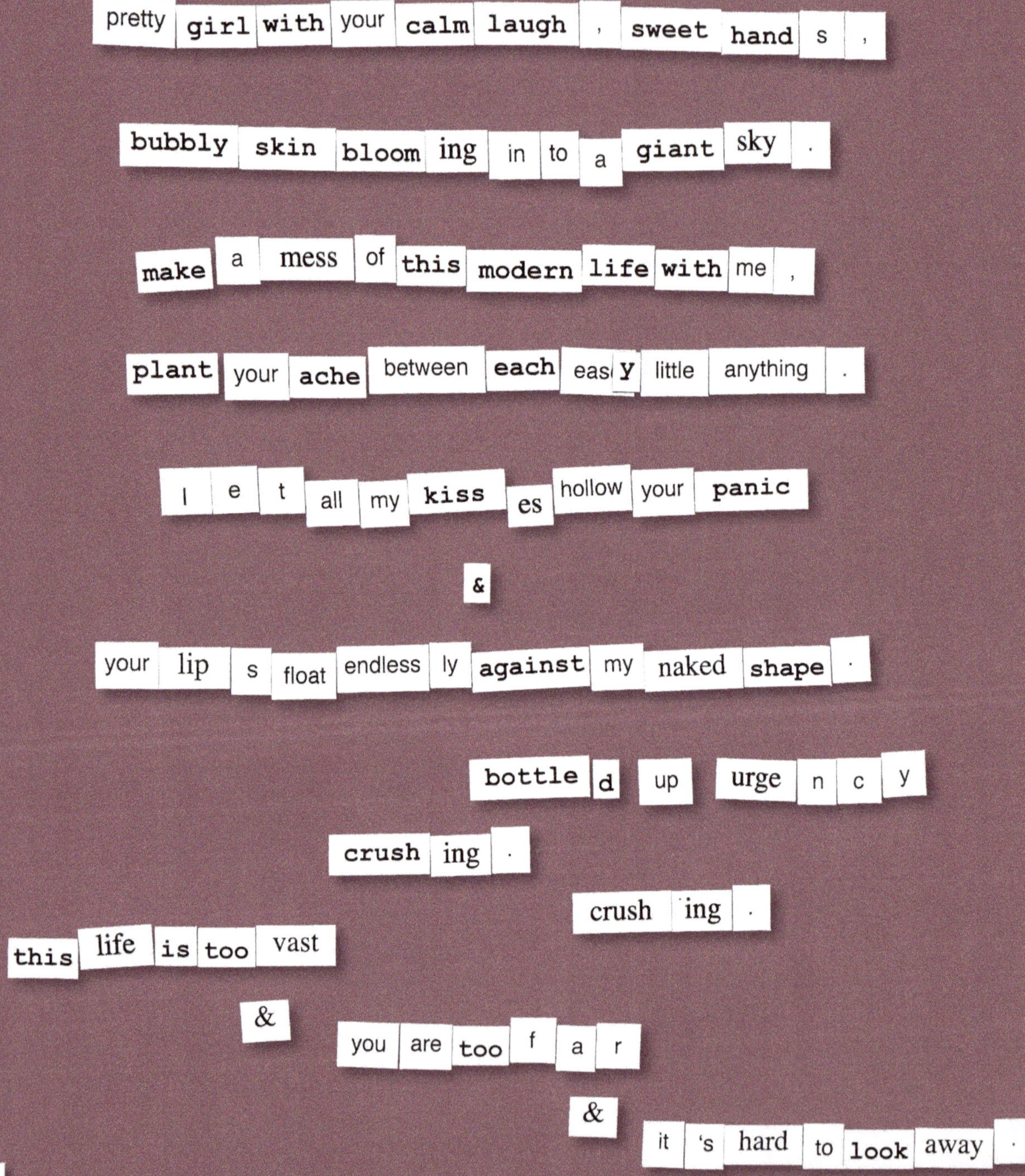

pretty girl with your calm laugh , sweet hand s ,
bubbly skin bloom ing in to a giant sky .
make a mess of this modern life with me ,
plant your ache between each eas y little anything .
l e t all my kiss es hollow your panic
&
your lip s float endless ly against my naked shape .
bottle d up urge n c y
crush ing .
crush ing .
this life is too vast
&
you are too f a r
&
it 's hard to look away .

red is

fingertip s carv ing against hot flesh ,

when you smile at me & O h , do I blush ,

an open flame throb b ing for wild er ness ,

my lipstick caught on your neck ,

the wine on a ghost s breath ,

my high heels ach ing at my feet for relief ,

romance

my sheets

a mad woman

this dress

my sappy heart

intoxicate d

a fever

young love

to bleed

old love , too

I am a growl ing feminist with ferocious rage

and a feline reputation . my heart know s sorrow ,

but remember s how to swell on good day s .

I am sultry & sexy & home is where I am .

I ooze Romance & I wrap my ego in a quiet pray er .

I trust she s in good hand s . I am several

idea s , both silly and stupid , zing and zip ,

sizzle sizzle sizzle .

I am alive , an open roar , smooth marble .

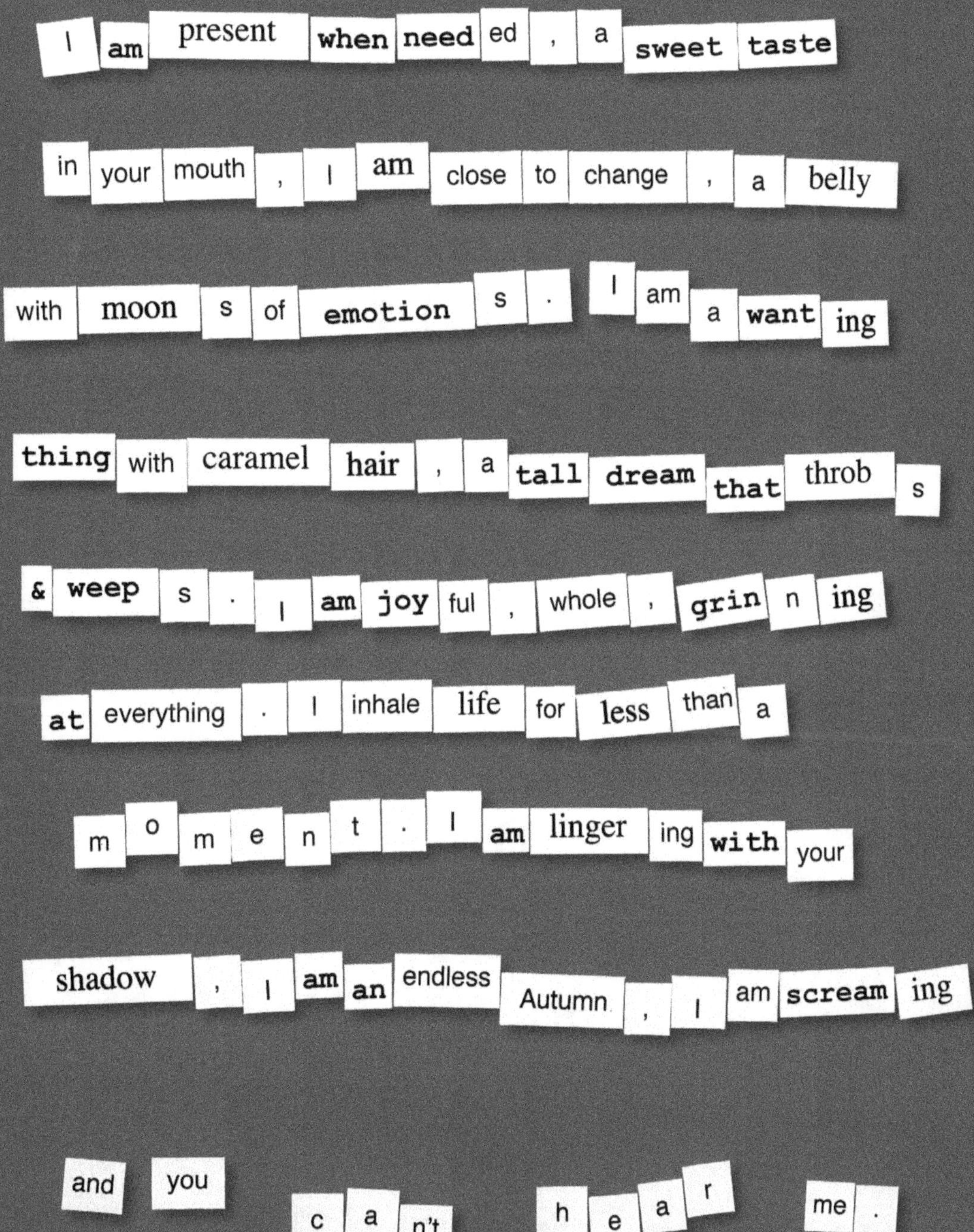

I am present when needed , a sweet taste
in your mouth , I am close to change , a belly
with moons of emotions . I am a wanting
thing with caramel hair , a tall dream that throbs
& weeps . I am joyful , whole , grinning
at everything . I inhale life for less than a
moment . I am lingering with your
shadow , I am an endless Autumn , I am screaming
and you can't hear me .

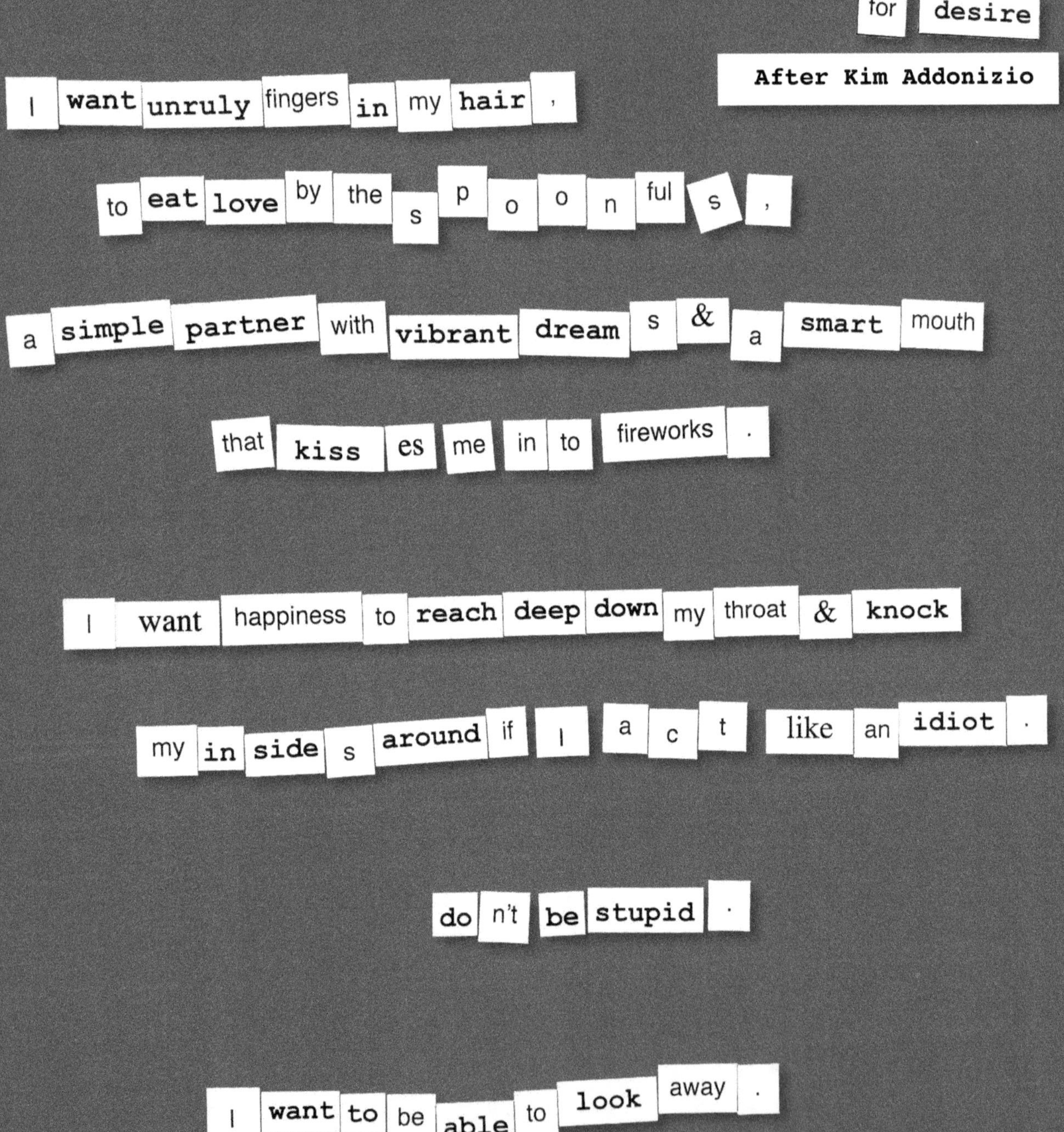

for desire

After Kim Addonizio

I want unruly fingers in my hair,

to eat love by the spoonfuls,

a simple partner with vibrant dreams & a smart mouth

that kisses me into fireworks.

I want happiness to reach deep down my throat & knock

my insides around if I act like an idiot.

don't be stupid.

I want to be able to look away.

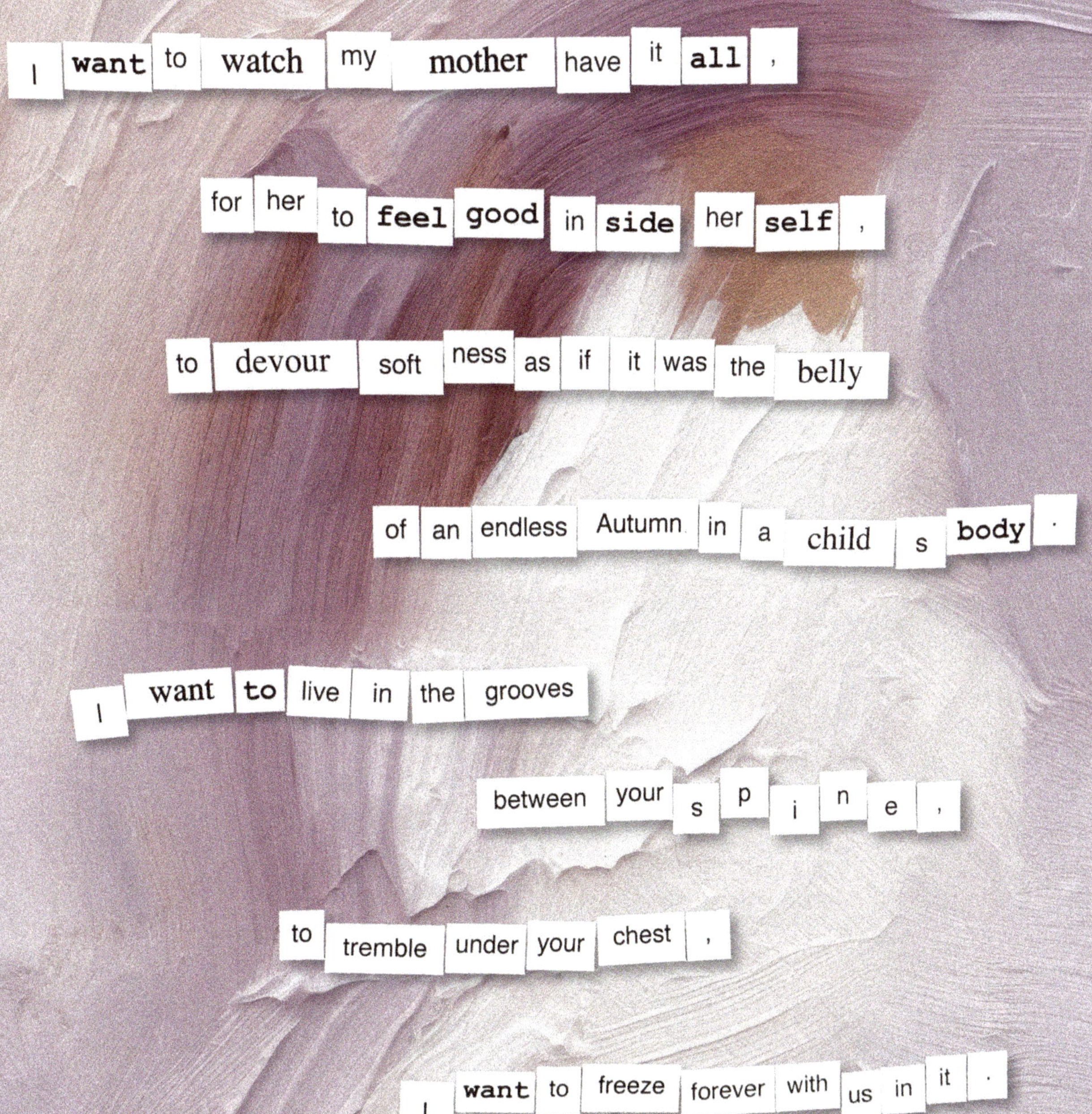

I want to watch my mother have it all ,

for her to feel good in side her self ,

to devour soft ness as if it was the belly

of an endless Autumn in a child s body .

I want to live in the grooves

between your s p i n e ,

to tremble under your chest ,

I want to freeze forever with us in it .

I want fruit r i p e as morning breath ,

to wake young & un afraid of the world .

I want to admire everything without remorse ,

to ache without be ing crush ed .

I want to feel the h o l e s in my body

with out f e e l ing broken .

when she is in love

she choose s the heels ,

f e e l s sexy naked ,

drink s the good wine ,

has the voice of a c a n y o n

deep

l o w .

she love s with bold ness between her hip s ,

and clear affection .

all of her giant love roar s in to a

long slip of worship .

when she is in love

she feels a soft home in every vessel,

safe and full bloom.

she growls and rumbles loud, she exists as

more than a shadow.

she loves with all of her skin, and a heart too fragile.

her love melts the darkness, won't fall apart,

and breathes longingly.

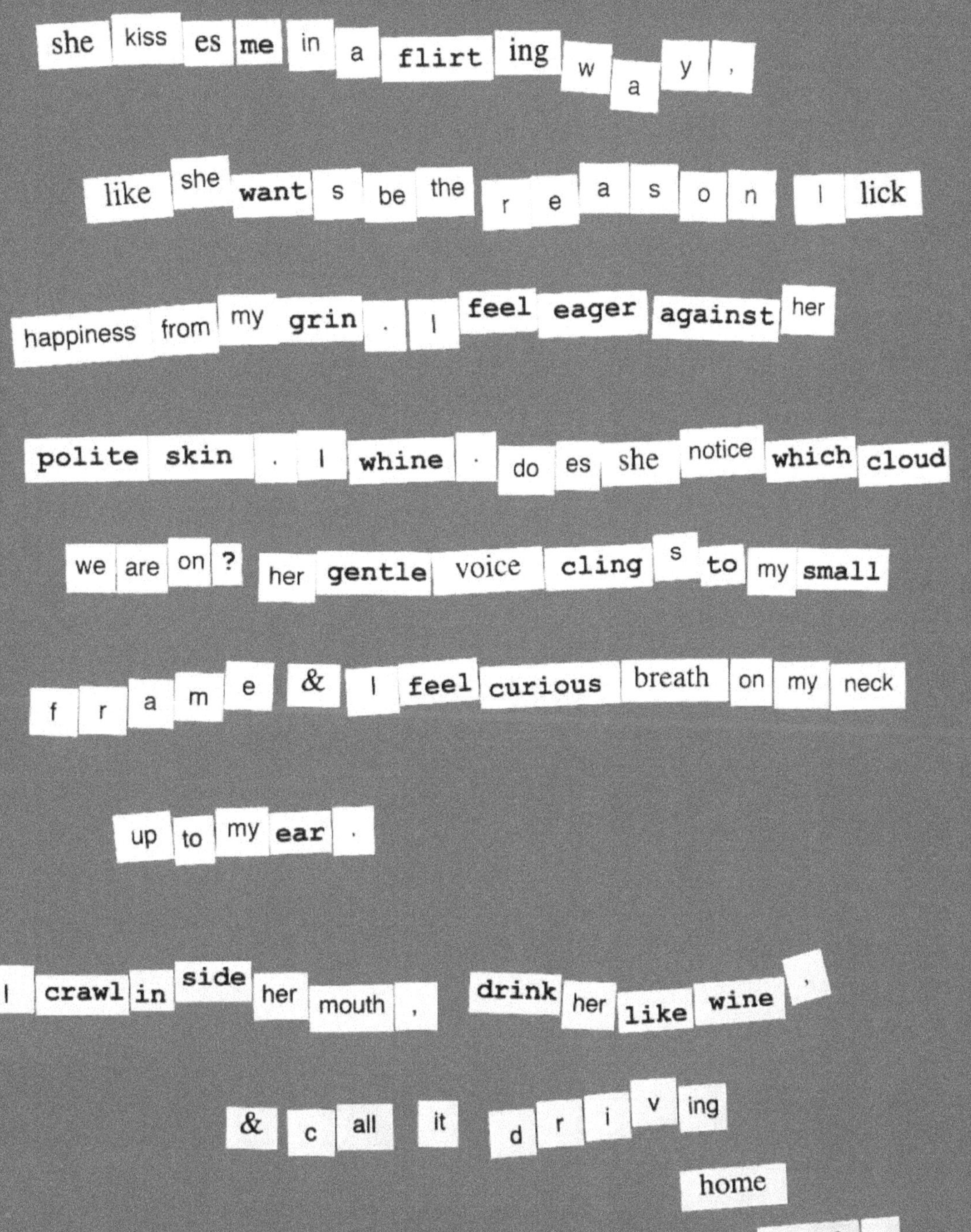

she kiss es me in a flirt ing way ,
like she want s be the reason I lick
happiness from my grin . I feel eager against her
polite skin . I whine . do es she notice which cloud
we are on ? her gentle voice cling s to my small
f r a m e & I feel curious breath on my neck
up to my ear .
I crawl in side her mouth , drink her like wine '
& c all it d r i v ing
home
drunk .

my favorites
filth y sun
devour my laughter
loudmouth
August
&
honey
summer
romance
chocolate
fever
lipstick
sloppy grin
tongue
rack
euphoric
.
hip
booty
throat
neck
gay
between
lesbian s
want
want
want
high
hollow ache
oopsie-daisy
ménage á trois
apparatus
bare
body
candy cane drool
earth-shattering
,
uuurrrrppp

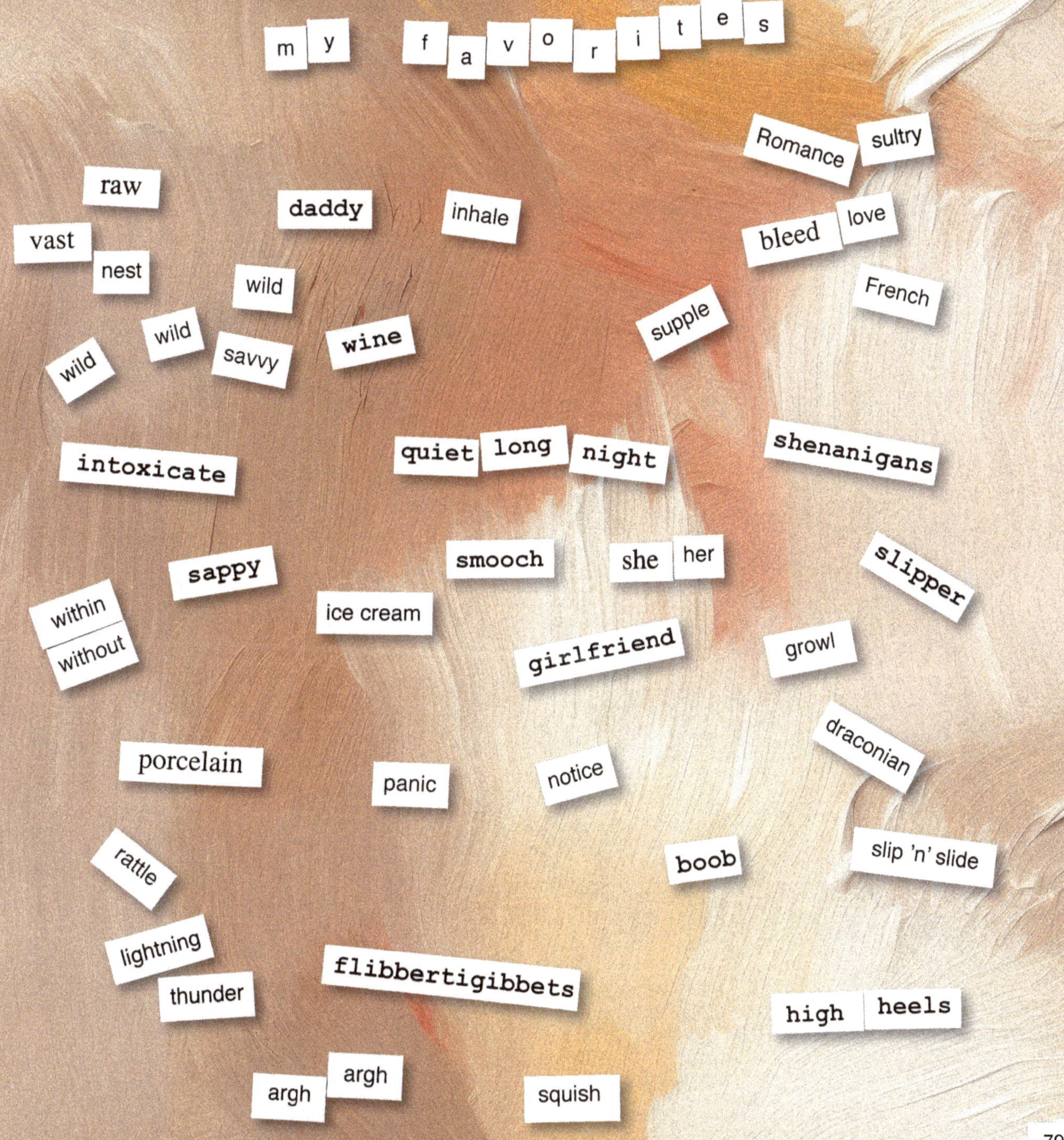

my favorites
raw
vast
nest
daddy
inhale
Romance sultry
bleed love
wild
French
wild
wild
savvy
wine
supple
intoxicate
quiet long night
shenanigans
sappy
smooch she her
slipper
within
without
ice cream
girlfriend
growl
porcelain
panic
notice
draconian
rattle
boob
slip 'n' slide
lightning
thunder
flibbertigibbets
high heels
argh argh
squish
79

word search

shadow
Romance
sultry
raw
ratchet
daddy
inhale
pain
ferocious
bleed
love
vast
humility
weight
nest
French
wild
wine
chocolate
supple
fashion
wild
wild
savvy
life
woman
wild
black
thing
intoxicate
misery
quiet
long
night
shenanigans
quarrel
baby
mad
sappy
smooch
she
her
slipper
within
ice cream
pretentious
without
girlfriend
growl
modesty
born
enthusiastically
underperformance
draconian
intelligent
porcelain
animal
notice
liquid
panic
rattle
mother
sausage
fever
boob
slip 'n' slide
heal
lightning
marble
summer
thunder
flibbertigibbets
high
heels
hunger
drool
caramel
explore
argh
argh
squish

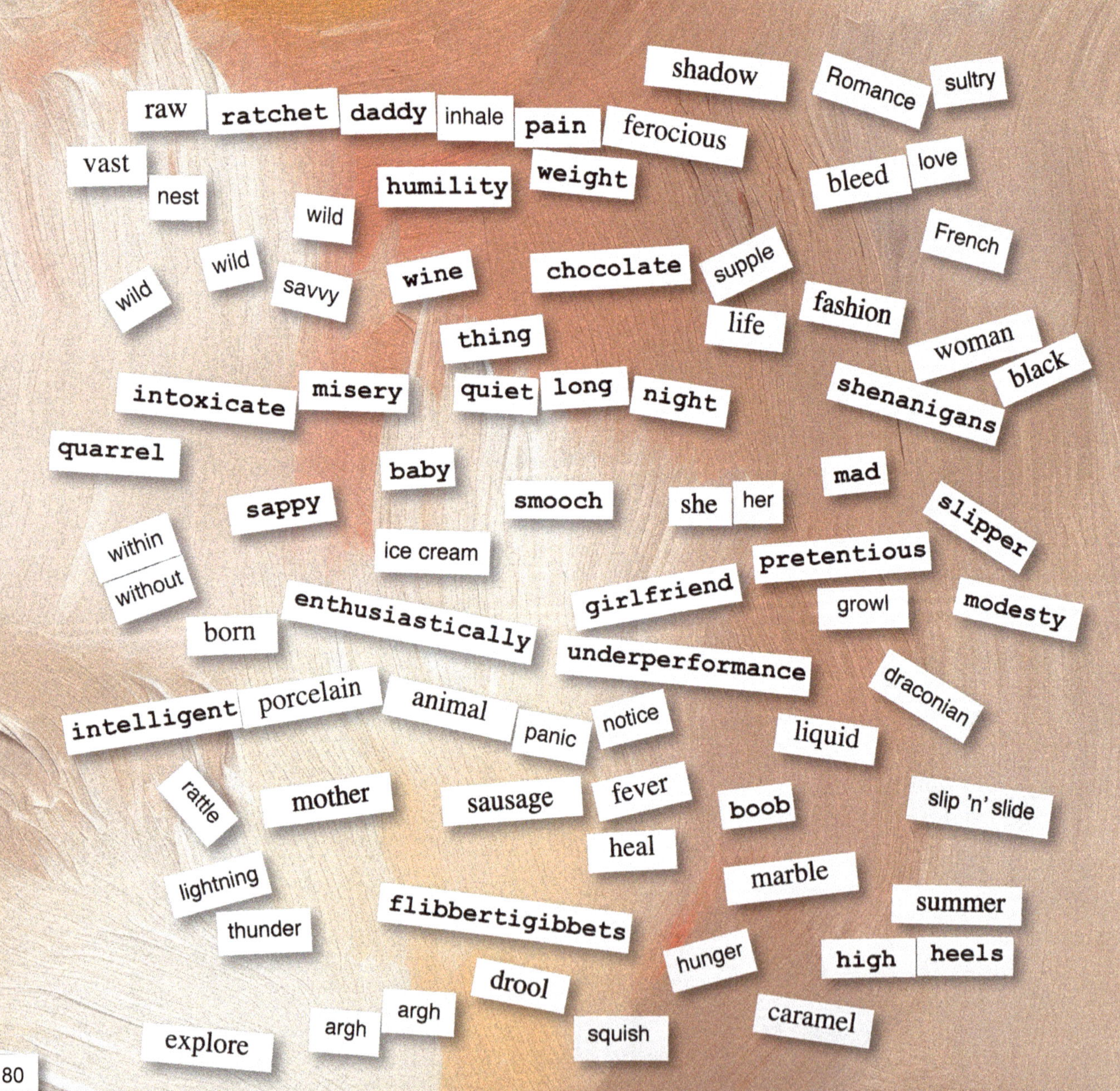

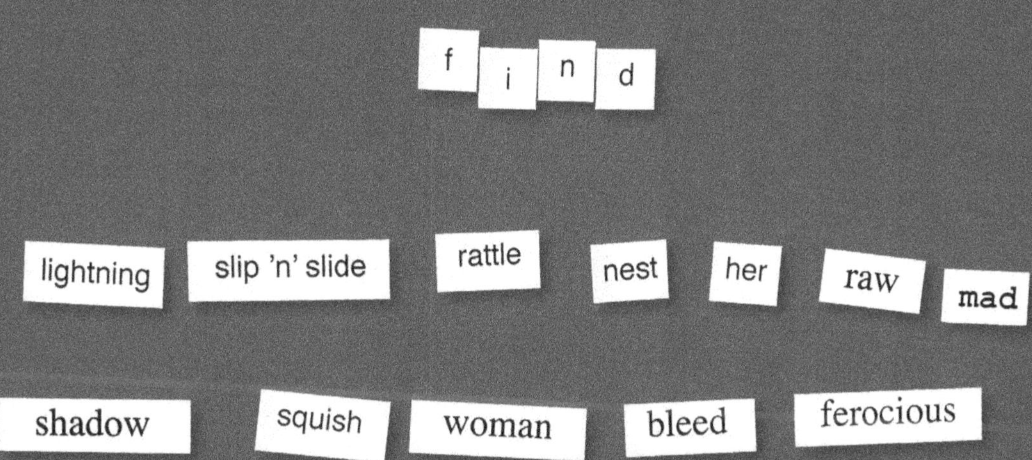

find
lightning   slip 'n' slide   rattle   nest   her   raw   mad
shadow   squish   woman   bleed   ferocious

Acknowledgements

I'd like to thank my mother for raising me to be thick-skinned,
yet soft hearted, I would never have the passion to write this
book without your constant guidance. You will always be the
reason I am who I am.

To anyone that has read my poetry or either of my other books.
You will always hold a special place in my heart. I hope this
books finds a safe place in your heart to nurture you and help
you grow in this world.

To Natalie Durman for always helping me with my titles.
You save lives.

To Amy Kay for constantly having the best prompts and for
letting me write my heart out, for being such an inspiration.
So many of these prompts were inspired by her and her work.

To Monica, Angelica, and Arya. You three are the greatest
friends I'll ever have. Thank you for always being there and for
letting me fall, but for helping pick me back up when I do.
I love you three so big.

To my Instagram friends, I love you. Every single one of you.
You know who you are.

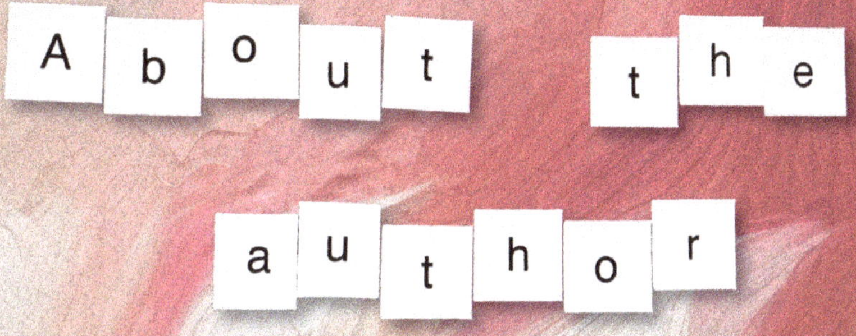

Casey Merkley is a poet/author residing in Indiana.
She started sharing her writing in 2018 and shortly
after, made an Instagram account specifically for her
writings. An eternity of everythings was her debut
poetry collection, and to taste you in another form is her
second with September makes a mess of me being her
third. she hopes this book teaches you about love, loss,
and the art of holding on tightly in this manic world.
In her spare time, you can find her in a world of her own
at her typewriter mending hearts as she goes.

Email: Casey_merkley@yahoo.com
Instagram: Ladyleopoetry